American Culture

IN WATER, BLOOD, OIL & BREAD

Kenneth Walley

⊛IBUNET
Publishing

Published by
Cibunet Publishing
P. O. Box 444
Woodlawn, NY 10470
Email: admin@cibunet.com
Website: www.cibunet.com

TABLE OF CONTENTS

CHAPTER FOUR

CHAPTER FIVE

CHAPTER SIX

CHAPTER SEVEN

CHAPTER EIGHT

CHAPTER NINE

CHAPTER TEN

INTRODUCTION

Within the last two hundred years North America has experienced rapid cultural transformations that have impacted the rest of the world significantly. As the giant melting pot of all cultures, American culture is a microcosm of how the whole world is evolving spiritually and socio-economically.

History records that several Christian religious groups emigrated from Europe to the United States between the seventeenth and nineteenth century. The Puritans were among the first group of migrants to settle in North America. The Puritans were part of the Church of England that sought to eliminate the practices of the Roman Catholic Church from which the Church of England originated. They settled down primarily in the Massachusetts area and spread into Rhode Island, Connecticut and elsewhere. The Puritans sought to practice a purer form of Christianity as part of their motivation for emigrating from England and this remained core to their heartbeat. Most of the founding fathers of this nation were active participants in their local Christian Churches and so their faith weighed in heavily in the draft of the constitution. Though they were not attempting to set up a religious state, their belief in God and the liberties of Christ's mission to mankind was at the forefront of their thinking.

To ensure that the conscience of the nation was undergirded with sound values, the justice system used 'oath upon the bible' to hold people accountable, the Ten Commandments was posted at public buildings and prayer was said to invoke God at public ceremonies and in schools. These were all systemic steps to make people uphold the high moral standards enshrined in the scriptures.

Today the storyline has changed dramatically. Proponents of a society devoid of God have worked hard to have the Ten Commandments removed from public buildings and the practice of prayer taken out of public schools.

The Ten Commandments were a compressed version of approximately six hundred divine rules that were given to Moses. Knowledge of these ten rules was intended to establish the fundamental premise for guiding human culture. Water, blood, oil and bread are metaphors of the four progressive ways by which God facilitates our humanity to flourish. Water is significant of how God's word is designed to wash us so we become sanctified. Blood is how we become dedicated to God through the blood of Jesus that was shed on the cross of Calvary for the remission of our sins. Oil is significant of how God anoints us with unique abilities. Bread is the ultimate providence of God for our sustenance.

1

The Culture of Inspiration

"You shall have no other gods before Me"
Exodus 20:3

At airports, on the train, bus, sitting at the park and elsewhere you would find a lot of people deeply engrossed in either watching something entertaining or news on their devices, reading, listening or texting. During my teenage years I spent roughly a third of my time watching television. My parents often came back home late from work and so after school it was 'Sesame street', followed by 'Cartoon Network's 'Tom and Jerry' and so on, then Soap Operas and finally the late-night movies. At the time I gave my life to Christ, all my free time was already taken. I was constantly watching television when not attending classes or doing school work. God wanted access to the tube of my soul, so he convicted me not to turn on my television for a season.

Today our choices are more sophisticated with news channels, sports, drama, comedy, romance, action, adventure genres available non-stop by subscription. The radio and internet are among other tubes of access to our soul. There is a fierce competition by spiritual, demonic and human forces for the soul of this generation. Jesus told the Church in Laodicea – "Behold, I stand at the door and knock. If anyone hears My voice and opens the door, I will come in to him and dine with him, and he with Me. To him who overcomes I will grant to sit with Me on My throne, as I also overcame and sat down with My Father on His throne. "He who has an ear, let him hear what the Spirit says to the churches" Revelations 3:20-22. Jesus is knocking on the door of our hearts for access to the tube of our soul. The first commandment is the essence of who inspires us. Inspire is a word that originally draws from two root words, 'in' and 'spirit'. It is how we are stimulated from the spirit realm to live our lives, do things, go places and so on.

Joshua led the Israelites to take possession of the Promised Land and this was followed by several other judges who administered the affairs of the young nation. During the era of Samuel, the prophet who became the last judge, the Israelites requested for a king to be installed over the nation. Saul from the tribe of Benjamin was chosen and anointed over Israel. Samuel was the kingmaker who fostered the transition of Israel's government into a monarchy. While still serving as God's prophet to Israel, God sends Samuel with an assignment for King Saul to completely destroy the Amalekites. The ancestors of these Amalekites had engaged the Israelites in a brutal war during their journey from Egypt and so God had decided to make war with them until they were completely annihilated. King Saul accepted the assignment but executed it in his own way. Contrary to the instructions, he destroyed whatever was of 'no value' to him and preserved Agag the Amalekite king as well as whatever he considered of value. Samuel visits King Saul after the mission and rebukes him.

"And Samuel said, Hath the LORD as great delight in burnt offerings and sacrifices, as in obeying the voice of the LORD? Behold, to obey is better than sacrifice, and to hearken than the fat of rams. For rebellion is as the sin of witchcraft, and stubbornness is as iniquity and idolatry. Because thou hast rejected the word of the LORD, he hath also rejected thee from being king" 2 Samuel 15:22&23

Samuel uses these words to describe the actions of King Saul - Obey (Disobey), Hearken (Ignore), Rebellion as Witchcraft, Stubbornness as Iniquity (Wickedness) and Idolatry. While disobedience, ignorance, rebellion, stubbornness and wickedness are character traits that may be associated with anyone whether religious or not, witchcraft and idolatry are deep spiritual vices.

Witchcraft was used here in the sense of divination or consulting with demon spirits, while idolatry is the worship of demon spirits behind so called 'gods'. The consequence of witchcraft and idolatry is the influence of demon spirits upon people. People who are ignorant of God, disobedient to His Word, rebellious, stubborn and wicked are usually under the influence of demonic spirits.

There is a progressive nuance with the words ignorance, disobedience, rebellion, stubbornness and wickedness. Ignorance is failure to learn about God. Disobedience is to abstain from fulfilling God's word to us. Rebellion is to turn our hearts away from the inspiration of God. Stubbornness is to remain in a hard-hearted attitude towards God. Wickedness is to demonstrate such apathy towards our fellow man

The moment our hearts are turned away from God, we automatically become exposed to all other spirits of devils that want to influence our lives contrary to God's will. The human spirit is like the antennae of a radio or television set which pick up signals from a transmitting station. You can turn to any channel that you desire to receive broadcasts. If you turn the channel of your spirit to God, then you receive divine

16

inspiration. Whenever we turn our channel away from God, our human spirit contacts spirits of idolatry and Witchcraft.

Water of the Conscience

The Great Awakening was a protestant and evangelical revival movement that took place from 1730 to 1755. Around this time revivalists such as Jonathan Edwards, George Whitefield and Samuel Davies impacted the landscape of America's spirituality. They emphasized a departure from the ritualistic and liturgical practices of Christianity while encouraging Christians to develop a vibrant personal relationship with God through salvation in Jesus Christ. They encouraged white slave owners to educate their African American slaves, so they would be able to read the bible. Overall the Great Awakening fostered a new culture among Christians who now begun to study the scriptures at home and develop their insight of God.

There are a new generation of leaders and people in America that have blatantly ignored the role of God in the founding of this nation. It is obvious that the nation is in a freefall of spiritual, moral and socio-economic decline. "Hear the word of the LORD, ye children of Israel: for the LORD hath a controversy with the inhabitants of the land, because there is no truth, nor mercy, nor knowledge of God in the land… My people are destroyed for lack of knowledge: because thou hast rejected knowledge, I will also reject thee, that thou shalt be no priest to me: seeing thou hast forgotten the law of thy God, I will also forget thy children" Hosea 4:1&6. The conscience of man is the seat of his value system. It is like a bank which holds our values of right and wrong as well as good and evil. We are all born with an empty conscience. "Foolishness is bound in the heart of a child; but the rod of correction shall drive it far from him" Proverbs 22:15. The word 'foolishness' here is an expression for 'empty' while the 'rod of correction' signifies the word of God. God's word is like water that fills up the empty conscience of a child that is instructed with scriptures. Knowledge of God's word is the standard of right and wrong as well as good and evil for the conscience. Without these standards we become prone to a misplacement of what is fundamentally right or wrong as well as good or evil.

Whenever we receive any information our conscience filters them into two separate compartments where right and good occupy one compartment while wrong and evil occupy the other compartment. So long as fresh water is poured into the conscience, the standards are set in place and the filters of the conscience work properly. When you deliberately pour dirty water into a purification tank the filters become quickly clogged. In the same way constantly exposing the conscience to corrupt information makes the conscience weak. The only way to keep our conscience pure is to constantly let in the fresh water of God's word. The Apostle Paul mentions a severe condition of the conscience in 1 Timothy 4:2 "Speaking lies in hypocrisy; having their conscience seared with a hot iron." To understand this scripture, we have to take a look at tabernacle of Moses where the conscience is represented as the Brazen Laver. It was made of highly polished brass that acted as a mirror to the worshipper. Imagine that someone takes a hot iron and whacks this mirror. It is no longer possible to see a good reflection of oneself in this mirror. A conscience seared with a hot iron is one that looks like a broken mirror. The reason being that such a person knowing what is right and good decides to transpose such information into the compartment of wrong and evil. When this happens, the conscience can no longer function as God intended. Any generation of people that fail to learn God's word would end up veering away from the standards of a good conscience. Moral wrongs and evil become prevalent in society and the consequences are passed on from one generation to another.

Blood of the Emotion

The Second Great Awakening in America took place during the period from 1800 to the 1830s. This awakening was characterized by an increased enthusiasm and emotion for spiritual awareness. There was an overall increase in evangelistic outreaches to the unsaved and so many people gave their lives to Christ. Evangelism is how we inspire the world with the gospel of salvation. The redemptive work of Jesus Christ on the cross of Calvary becomes a reality for those who are convicted. Sinners have an opportunity to receive Jesus Christ into their lives and the blood of Jesus cleanses them from their sins.

The emotion is our connection to the environment. Our sense of sight, hearing, smell, taste and touch are all connected to our emotions. Whatever information we gather from our environment is subjected to our value system in the conscience. The conscience determines if such information falls into the category of right and good or wrong and evil. The emotion is different from the conscience because it is the seat of our instincts. While we are born with an empty conscience, the instincts carry information of the bloodline. We inherit traits of our ancestors through the bloodline. In any aspect of life where our ancestors upheld divine values, there is a great chance that we may also uphold such values and vice versa. This means that we all have the tendency to manifest some of the negative character traits of our ancestors in our instincts. "Let no man say when he is tempted, I am tempted of God: for God cannot be tempted with evil, neither tempteth he any man: But every man is tempted, when he is drawn away of his own lust, and enticed. Then when lust hath conceived, it bringeth forth sin: and sin, when it is finished, bringeth forth death" James 1:13-15.

Lust is like eggs that are inherited ancestrally and reside in the bloodline. The tempter recognizes lust in a person's bloodline and can entice them. In the same way a sperm hatches the egg in the womb of a female, the tempter can conceive with the lust in a person to birth sin. The question here is, how can one be free from lusts that are inherent in one's bloodline? The blood of Jesus Christ is our source of redemption from ancestral lusts that inhibit us. Any aspect of life where we find out that we are powerless to uphold God's word indicates inherent lust. Some pathological issues, some addictive behaviors, some chronic diseases and incurable infirmities fall into this category. Bloodline issues are responsible for so many people in society who are incarcerated for crimes that they were powerless to resist, premature death from incurable infirmities, severe addictions and many more. The sacrifice of Jesus Christ on the cross of Calvary gives us access to the blood of redemption. The blood of Jesus redeems us from ancestral sins so that we can live free from the inhibitions of our bloodline. God's grace is unleashed on those who repent from their sins and seek forgiveness through the cleansing power of the blood of Jesus. Grace empowers us to overcome the inherent lusts that enslave us to demonic dominance. Salvation in Christ affords people the opportunity to experience the redemptive power of the blood of Jesus Christ.

Oil of the Intellect

The Third Great Awakening took place from around 1850 into the early part of the twentieth century. It was characterized by the manifestations of the gifts of the Holy Spirit including speaking in tongues as well as other signs, healings and miracles. This was during a period when the economy of the United States was in crisis, many businesses were not thriving and many people were unemployed. Christians across the nation gathered everywhere there was a revival meeting and sought God prayerfully. When revival came through, it was more profound on Azusa Street where a small fellowship of believers was graced with the outpouring of the Holy Spirit. People travelled from all over the United States and across the world to receive the experience. This was the Third Great Awakening at which time Pentecostal Churches sprung up across the nation, denominations like Assemblies of God and Church of God were birthed. Christian educational institutions were established across the country and many missionaries travelled out of the United States to establish missions globally.

The intellect is the faculty of the mind for thoughts or reasoning. Here we process information based on conscience values, emotional dispositions and facts. Apart from these three components of an intelligent decision, other factors that determine the outcome of our thought process are our gifts and talents. The spiritual gifts and talents are considered the anointing of God within us. It is God's oil that furnishes us with the wisdom of God in specific areas of life where we are particularly endowed. Prayer ignites our spiritual gifts and enhances our awareness of creativity potentials.

Bread of the Will

The Fourth Great Awakening is the period from 1960 through the 1980's. At this time God granted the wisdom to grow small churches, enterprises and institutions into mega-scale entities. Churches developed systems of effective discipleship such as the cell group structure while corporate enterprises cultivated franchising as a strategy for expansive growth. Mega ministries such as Oral Roberts, Kenneth Hagin, Kenneth Copeland, Jerry Savelle, Jimmy Swaggart, Dr. David Yonggi Cho etc. became prominent during the Fourth Great Awakening.

The cell group was a discipleship system that made it possible to be a part of a large Church and yet enjoy the benefits of interactions with a close-knit group. Though He had a large following during His earthly ministry, Jesus Christ selected twelve of his followers to become an inner group of disciples. He had a more interactive relationship with this group of twelve and they formed the core leadership of the New Testament Church.

It is the same concept that drives the franchise model of enterprises. New business owners do not want to go through the long struggle of developing a unique brand. This could take decades of teething pain. Rather they pay to become the franchise owner of a well-established brand. This way they benefit from easy name recognition and consequent patronage of those already familiar with the brand. In any new environment the human mind more readily adapts with those things that are familiar before venturing with the unknown.

The will is the faculty of the mind where our actions are initiated. In whatever direction our will dictates is where we follow. The will is where we make our determinations after processing our values, sentiments and facts. Ultimately it is the direction of our inclinations that determines what we do as well as how we earn a living. Whether we are poor or rich is often a direct consequence of how we invest ourselves on a consistent basis.

If our determinations and what we do begin to flourish, then multiplication or branching out becomes our next inclination. We develop manuals from the processes by which we have experienced results so that others who join us can apply these same processes. If the root inspiration for any of our systemic processes is godly or demonic, then it gets perpetuated from generation to generation.

2

The Culture of Truth

*"You shall not make for yourself a carved image—any
likeness of anything that is in heaven above, or that is in the
earth beneath, or that is in the water under the earth; you shall
not bow down to them nor serve them"*
Exodus 20:4&5a

America's socio-political structure lends itself to the
Roman culture which was built upon the heritage of
the Greeks, Persians and Babylonians. We can trace
the democratic system of government, architecture,
education, philosophy and several institutions to these
historic foundations. The New Testament was written
at the peak of the Roman era. The challenges of the
Roman world which are apparently present in
American society today was addressed by the Apostle
Paul in his letter to the Romans. The Apostle Paul

lends from the second commandment as he writes in Romans 1:18-32, "For the wrath of God is revealed from heaven against all ungodliness and unrighteousness of men, who suppress the truth in unrighteousness, because what may be known of God is manifest in them, for God has shown it to them. For since the creation of the world His invisible attributes are clearly seen, being understood by the things that are made, even His eternal power and Godhead, so that they are without excuse, because, although they knew God, they did not glorify Him as God, nor were thankful, but became futile in their thoughts, and their foolish hearts were darkened. Professing to be wise, they became fools, and changed the glory of the incorruptible God into an image made like corruptible man—and birds and four-footed animals and creeping things. Therefore, God also gave them up to uncleanness, in the lusts of their hearts, to dishonor their bodies among themselves, who exchanged the truth of God for the lie, and worshiped and served the creature rather than the Creator, who is blessed forever. Amen. For this reason, God gave them up to vile passions. For even their women exchanged the natural use for what is against nature. Likewise, also the men, leaving the natural use of the woman, burned in their lust for one another, men with men committing what is shameful, and receiving in themselves the penalty of their error which was due. And even as they did not like to retain God in their knowledge, God gave them over to a debased mind, to do those things which are not fitting; being filled with all unrighteousness, sexual immorality, wickedness, covetousness, maliciousness; full of envy, murder, strife, deceit, evil-mindedness; they are whisperers, backbiters, haters of God, violent, proud, boasters, inventors of evil things, disobedient to parents, undiscerning, untrustworthy, unloving, unforgiving, unmerciful; who, knowing the righteous judgment of God, that those who practice such things are deserving of death, not only do the same but also approve of those who practice them."

The Apostle Paul unveils the fundamental ways by which we come to the knowledge of truth, which are:

1. Divine Principles/Generational Logos-word
2. Divine Revelation/Ancestral Rhema-word
3. Divine Anointing/Natural Science
4. Divine Covenants/Relational

The root of all error is the attempt to eliminate any of the core sources of truth from truth. Truth is generational, revelatory, scientific and relational. The Apostle Paul warns the Colossian Church to beware of any attempts to subvert the foundations of truth because it is a ploy by which the kingdom of darkness attempts to rob God's children of their heritage in Christ: "Beware lest anyone cheat you through philosophy and empty deceit, according to the tradition of men, according to the basic principles of the world, and not according to Christ. For in Him dwells all the fullness of the Godhead bodily; and you are complete in Him, who is the head of all principality and power. In Him you were also circumcised with the circumcision made without hands, by putting off the body of the sins of the flesh, by the circumcision of Christ, buried with Him in baptism, in which you also were raised with Him through faith in the working of God, who raised Him from the dead. And you, being dead in your trespasses and the uncircumcision of your flesh, He has made alive together with Him, having forgiven you all trespasses, having wiped out the handwriting of requirements that was against us, which was contrary to us. And He has taken it out of the way, having nailed it to the cross. Having disarmed principalities and powers, He made a public spectacle of them, triumphing over them in it" Colossians 2:8-15. Through a relationship with Christ Jesus we are empowered to overcome the devices by which the kingdom of darkness keeps us under their domination.

Worldly Rudiments versus Divine Principles (Generational Logos-Word)

Worldly rudiments are principles upheld by secular society that are not in agreement with God's word as taught in the scriptures. Such rudiments are those that brazenly or subtly deny the existence of God, oppose the standards of righteousness, salvation, faith and eternal life in Christ Jesus. Furthermore, such rudiments that seek to replace godliness with humanism by suggesting we are our own gods, pluralism that suggests every religion must be accepted as a way to God, materialism that suggests the achievement of riches as the ultimate goal of man and the redefinition of morality in perverse ways. Essentially a worldly principle denies the God-factor of our existence. When we uphold a worldly principle as truth, it enslaves us in bondage to Satan and weakens our effectiveness as humans. "Even so we, when we were children, were in bondage under the elements of the world" Galatians 4:3.

The scriptures however serve as the foundation of whatever qualifies to be truth. Consisting of information handed down by oral tradition,

31

revelation, facts and testimonials, the scriptures represent truths which have been carefully documented by generations of distinguished people with a burden to preserve truth in its purest form. "All Scripture is given by inspiration of God, and is profitable for doctrine, for reproof, for correction, for instruction in righteousness, that the man of God may be complete, thoroughly equipped for every good work" 2 Timothy 3:16. From time to time historians and archaeologists have continued to unravel evidence that give credence to these truths that are enshrined in the scriptures. The scriptures form the core litmus test for whatever may be classified as truth.

The story of King Nebuchadnezzar throws light on the efficacy of the scriptures manifesting the power of God. He had a dream in which he saw an image with a head of gold, chest of silver, thighs of brass, legs of iron with clay and a stone that crushes the entire image. Daniel interprets the dream as a revelation of eras of world dominance where King Nebuchadnezzar's reign of Babylon was depicted as the head of gold. King Nebuchadnezzar is not entirely pleased with the fact that there would be other kingdoms that rise into dominance after his reign, so he attempts to manipulate the revelation. He sets up an image made entirely of gold and summons everyone in the world under him to bow to this image. Shadrach, Meshach and Abednego were a part of his leadership but of Hebrew origin and they refused to bow down to the image. They were simply complying with the second commandment that prevented them from bowing down to a graven image. King Nebuchadnezzar instructed that they should be thrown in a furnace of fire that was heated seven times hotter than usual. Those who bound and threw Shadrach, Meshach and Abednego into the fire were consumed by the fire. "Then Nebuchadnezzar the king was astonished, and rose up in haste, and spake, and said unto his counsellors, Did not we cast three men bound into the midst of the fire? They answered and said unto the king, True, O king. He answered and said, Lo, I see four men loose, walking in the midst of the fire, and they have no hurt; and the form of the fourth is like the Son of God. Then Nebuchadnezzar came near to the mouth of the burning fiery furnace, and spake, and said, Shadrach, Meshach, and Abednego, ye servants of the Most High God, come forth, and come hither. Then Shadrach, Meshach, and Abednego, came forth of the midst of the fire. And the princes, governors, and captains, and the king's counselors, being gathered together, saw these men, upon whose bodies the fire had no power, nor was an hair of their head singed, neither were their coats changed, nor the smell of fire had passed on them. Then Nebuchadnezzar spake, and said, Blessed be the God of Shadrach, Meshach, and Abednego, who hath sent his angel, and delivered his servants that trusted in him, and have changed the king's word, and yielded their bodies, that they might not serve nor worship any god, except their own God. Therefore, I make a decree, That every people, nation, and language, which speak anything amiss against the God of Shadrach, Meshach, and Abednego, shall be cut in pieces, and their houses shall be made a dunghill: because there is no other God that can deliver after this sort" Daniel 3:24-29. Notice first of all that Nebuchadnezzar saw the Son of God freely walking with the three Hebrew men in the fire. Secondly, though the fire of the furnace consumed the executioners, it did not consume Shadrach, Meshach and Abednego. This manifestation underscores the truth that upholding God's precept in its purest form invokes the power of God that would prevail over all elements of His creation.

Deception versus Divine Revelation (Ancestral Rhema-Word)

Deception is a dishonest or fraudulent way of getting people to falter. It is employed to put others in the dark. Deception may be initiated through the transmission of lust from the kingdom of darkness into the atmosphere. "For we ourselves were also once foolish, disobedient, deceived, serving various lusts and pleasures, living in malice and envy, hateful and hating one another" Titus 3:3. Deception can be inherent whereby we receive information from demon spirits that may communicate with us through dreams and visions. Third party clairvoyants and diviners may also convey deception to us. Though a taboo in recent history, today, it is not uncommon to find sign posts of psychic practitioners on the Main Street of cities and towns across North America. "For thus says the Lord of hosts, the God of Israel: Do not let your prophets and your diviners who are in your midst deceive you, nor listen to your dreams which you cause to be dreamed. For they prophesy falsely to you in My name; I have not sent them, says the Lord" Jeremiah 29:8&9.

Usually deception is information in a specific form that tends to provide direction. It may be tailor-made for a particular person or group of people. Deception also may be a demonic or human calculation intended to derail from the natural path of truth and right. Just as Eve yielded to the deception of the devil through the serpent, a serial killer or pathological liar may all claim inspiration for their actions. Deception is a tool of interference used for manipulating the actions of people.

Revelation that comes from God brings specific direction for an individual or group of people.

Fundamentally, revelation knowledge which is the rhema-word always hinges on a scripture which is a generational logos-word. A rhema-word brings application knowledge to a logos-word. They are always in agreement and complement each other. A good premise for testing a rhema-word is to always ask God to provide scriptures that validate your dreams or visions. "Do not despise prophecies. Test all things; hold fast what is good. Abstain from every form of evil" 1 Thessalonians 5:20-22.

The ultimate ability to test the validity of a spiritual revelation is through discernment. Discernment is a function of our spiritual nostrils. It is the ability to distinguish God's spirit and demonic spirits. Through discernment we can tell when human manipulators are at work with a deceptive scheme. Our redemption by the blood of Jesus from the kingdom of darkness activates our discernment. To develop good discernment, we must consciously abstain from every appearance of evil. "Unto the pure all things are pure: but unto them that are defiled and unbelieving is nothing pure; but even their mind and conscience is defiled" Titus 1:15. We cannot deliberately indulge in falsehood, dishonest schemes and expect our discernment to remain pure.

Humanistic Philosophy versus Divine Anointing

The Declaration of Independence crafted for the United States by Thomas Jefferson says: 'We hold these truths to be self-evident, that all men are created equal, that they are endowed by their Creator with certain unalienable Rights, that among these are Life, Liberty and the pursuit of Happiness'. Thomas Jefferson declared himself to be an epicurean during his lifetime. Epicureans teach the philosophical doctrine of the pursuit of happiness as among other thoughts about life and liberty and so it is commonly said that he borrowed from this inclination. While as humans we are naturally inclined with a disposition to pursue happiness, it is an emotional state that may become a delusion if it defines our mantra of existence. Human philosophy is any reasoning about life that appeals to the mind as sensible though it may not necessarily align with the scriptures. The American society has become so intensely obsessed with human philosophy that it reigns supreme at the forefront of the American mindset. We seem to be extremely eager to fill the void of godly wisdom with the view point of human philosophers like Socrates,

37

Plato, Aristotle and others from predominantly the Greek era. While the development of some educational disciplines can be traced to the development of philosophy as a whole, the deep flaws in our civic, socio-economic and scientific advancements can also be attributed with it. The constant effort to extricate God from our existence is core to our human philosophical limitations. Though a lot has been accomplished through American ingenuity such as the invention of the electric bulb by Con Edison, alternating current induction motor by Nicola Tesla, airplane by the Wright Brothers, the personal computer by John Blankenbaker and so much more, today the general perception of the mantra of 'the pursuit of happiness' is highly misconstrued. Those who have pioneered great achievements through creativity and innovation were in pursuit of 'purpose' and not 'happiness'. Today many people practice vocations solely because the trend is that such jobs highly reward financially. The notion here is that if we have much money we can afford all the material goods and pleasures of life that make us happy.

The landscape of American ingenuity is fundamentally the quest for creativity and innovation. True science is the study of God's works through the lenses of His logos-word, rhema-word and the divine endowments that lie within us. The divine endowments flow through the ancestral bloodline of every family as the anointing. The first generation of people God created were endowed with the fatherhood anointing. "And Adah bore Jabal. He was the father of those who dwell in tents and have livestock. His brother's name was Jubal. He was the father of all those who play the harp and flute. And as for Zillah, she also bore Tubal-Cain, an instructor of every craftsman in bronze and iron..." Genesis 4:20-22. The word 'father' in this scripture is from the Hebrew word 'Av' and it means originator or creator. God endowed the first generation of people with the anointing for creativity and originating various professions. These fathers would then pass on the creativity insights they gained by reason of the anointing to their children and consequently to future generations.

The inherent anointing within us is also known as the wisdom of God. "For the message of the cross is foolishness to those who are perishing, but to us who are being saved it is the power of God. For it is written: "I will destroy the wisdom of the wise, And bring to nothing the understanding of the prudent." Where is the wise? Where is the scribe? Where is the disputer of this age? Has not God made foolish the wisdom of this world? For since, in the wisdom of God, the world through wisdom did not know God, it pleased God through the foolishness of the message preached to save those who believe. For Jews request a sign, and Greeks seek after wisdom; but we preach Christ crucified, to the Jews a stumbling block and to the Greeks foolishness, but to those who are called, both Jews and Greeks, Christ the power of God and the wisdom of God. Because the foolishness of God is wiser than men, and the weakness of God is stronger than men" 1 Corinthians 1:18-25. The anointing is the wisdom of God that is lacking in our medicine, economics, politics and technology that leaves us with after treatment side-effects that may be life-threatening in some cases, grand-scale poverty, political maladministration, industrial menaces and all other cancers of society.

Worldly Tradition versus Divine Covenant

A worldly tradition is established when a demonic inspired method is institutionalized in human society. Worldly tradition is often employed as a tool for nepotism. Nepotism means discrimination, favoritism, partiality, racism, segregation and class-culture. It is a divisive method by which those who are privileged seek to fence-off categories of people from benefiting from certain privileges. Nepotism is egocentric and feeds into a self-centered nature that cares less for the feelings of others. It fosters wickedness and greed that bears every resemblance of the devil. Just as much as the founding fathers consisted of Christians who sought to establish a society free from the tyrannical oppression of European style monarchies, there were also practicing occultists among those who shaped the country. Interjections of Freemasonry concepts in the design of the capital city structures of Washington D.C. and institutional alignments with the occult are a common claim with hard evidence. In the same way the pyramids of Egypt, the symmetrical layout of the Tenochtitlan city of the Aztecs were designed to align with astronomic bodies, the U.S. capital and its obelisk were all designed to align with certain belief systems that totally misrepresent God the creator of the universe. As a result today, the political landscape of government in the United States is nothing short of a total debacle!

Traditions that contradict God's word can potentially lead generations of people astray and yet they may never know the root. A worldly tradition is a misrepresentation of God that is weaved into our regular fabric of life. Protocols, rules and regulations are used to make them mandatory and so they become systemic. Jesus experienced constant confrontation for not upholding the humanistic traditions of his day. "Then the scribes and Pharisees who were from Jerusalem came to Jesus, saying, "Why do Your disciples transgress the tradition of the elders? For they do not wash their hands when they eat bread. He answered and said to them, "Why do you also transgress the commandment of God because of your tradition? For God commanded, saying, 'Honor your father and your mother'; and, 'He who curses father or mother, let him be put to death.' But you say, 'Whoever says to his father or mother, "Whatever profit you might have received from me is a gift to God"— then he need not honor his father or mother.' Thus you have made the commandment of God of no effect by your tradition. Hypocrites! Well did Isaiah prophesy about you, saying: 'These people draw near to Me with their mouth, And honor Me with their lips, But their heart is far from Me. And in vain they worship Me, Teaching as doctrines the commandments of men'" Matthew 15:1-9.

The Jewish religious leaders during the lifetime of Jesus formulated a lot of traditions by which they intended to regulate Jewish society. By their accusation they were trying to hold Jesus accountable to their own standards of spirituality. The problem here was that these traditions they had established were a deviation from God's word. At best they were a misrepresentation of God. Human traditions muzzle the power of God's word. They are illegal extensions that interfere with God's prerogative of covenant blessings. God reserves the right to enter into exclusive covenant relationship with individuals by giving them promises and requiring specific obedience. To whoever God makes a promise and requires obedience, a covenant relationship is established. For such a person and his progeny God's covenant requirements become their legitimate tradition.

3

The Culture of Reverence

*"You shall not take the name of the Lord your God in vain,
for the Lord will not hold him guiltless who
takes His name in vain"*
Exodus 20:7

Irreverence for the name of God is common place in
conversations, street-cussing lingo and entertainment.
Radio, television and movie producers that previously
censored foul language are subdued by the
proliferation and so there is currently little censoring.
Though there is a rating system in place that notifies
the public of strong language content, the reality is
that you would hardly find a movie to watch that has
no strong language content. It is so profound such
that you will often hear people for no apparent reason
invoke the precious name of our Lord and Savior or
interject the f-word between Jesus and Christ.

A name identifies the nature and character of an object or person. It distinguishes one person from another and can reflect one's reputation or abilities. Our knowledge of God's name begins with God's own identification of Himself to the patriarch Abraham as Jehovah El-Shaddai. "When Abram was ninety-nine years old, the Lord appeared to Abram and said to him, "I am Almighty God; walk before Me and be blameless. And I will make My covenant between Me and you, and will multiply you exceedingly." Then Abram fell on his face, and God talked with him, saying: "As for Me, behold, My covenant is with you, and you shall be a father of many nations. No longer shall your name be called Abram, but your name shall be Abraham; for I have made you a father of many nations. I will make you exceedingly fruitful; and I will make nations of you, and kings shall come from you. And I will establish My covenant between Me and you and your descendants after you in their generations, for an everlasting covenant, to be God to you and your descendants after you. Also I give to you and your descendants after you the land in which you are a stranger, all the land of Canaan, as an everlasting possession; and I will be their God."

And God said to Abraham: "As for you, you shall keep My covenant, you and your descendants after you throughout their generations. This is My covenant which you shall keep, between Me and you and your descendants after you: Every male child among you shall be circumcised; and you shall be circumcised in the flesh of your foreskins, and it shall be a sign of the covenant between Me and you. He who is eight days old among you shall be circumcised, every male child in your generations, he who is born in your house or bought with money from any foreigner who is not your descendant. He who is born in your house and he who is bought with your money must be circumcised, and My covenant shall be in your flesh for an everlasting covenant. And the uncircumcised male child, who is not circumcised in the flesh of his foreskin, that person shall be cut off from his people; he has broken My covenant."

Then God said to Abraham, "As for Sarai your wife, you shall not call her name Sarai, but Sarah shall be her name. And I will bless her and also give you a son by her; then I will bless her, and she shall be a mother of nations; kings of peoples shall be from her" Genesis 17:1-16

In this encounter with Abraham, God unveils His own name by which He would relate to Abraham, a new and proper name of Abraham as well as the proper name of Sarah. These names were fundamental to their covenant relationship. In this relationship, God promised to manifest as the Almighty and required Abraham to subscribe to circumcision. In practice, physical circumcision is the cutting of the foreskin of the male organ. It is spiritually significant today of our repentance from dead works. "Circumcise yourselves to the Lord, And take away the foreskins of your hearts, You men of Judah and inhabitants of Jerusalem, Lest My fury come forth like fire, And burn so that no one can quench it, Because of the evil of your doings" Jeremiah 4:4. We see clearly that at the point when God identifies Himself by a name to mankind, it is within the framework of a covenant by which He intends to demonstrate His surpassing might through us. The condition however is that we walk perfectly before him. Abraham who was previously named 'Abram' which means 'exalted father' is given the name 'Abraham' which means 'father of many nations'. What a tremendous boost to his identity! The name Abraham is not only a reflection of his identity in the eyes of God his creator but also a reflection of the promises of God to him. Sarah's new name is also a reflection of God's promises for which reason her barren condition would be alleviated.

We get a deeper understanding of God's might in the encounter with Moses at the burning bush. During this encounter, God assigns Moses with the responsibility of bringing the Israelites out of Egypt. Upon hearing the assignment, Moses asks God a question – "Then Moses said to God, "Indeed, when I come to the children of Israel and say to them, 'The God of your fathers has sent me to you,' and they say to me, 'What is His name?' what shall I say to them?" And God said to Moses, "I AM WHO I AM." And He said, "Thus you shall say to the children of Israel, 'I AM has sent me to you'" Moreover God said to Moses, "Thus you shall say to the children of Israel: 'The Lord God of your fathers, the God of Abraham, the God of Isaac, and the God of Jacob, has sent me to you. This is My name forever, and this is My memorial to all generations'" Exodus 3:13-15. This is the first divine encounter of Moses and since he was not a leader in the Israelite community he needed to establish the identity of God. God unveils a new identity that builds upon the relationship with Israel's ancestors Abraham, Isaac and Jacob. The name 'I AM THAT I AM' unveils the omnipotence of God in ways beyond any human imagination. It signifies that as humans we would always be limited to how much God decides to unveil His unlimited potentials to us.

The Apostle Paul says of Him in Romans 11:33 – "Oh, the depth of the riches both of the wisdom and knowledge of God! How unsearchable are His judgments and His ways past finding out!" Throughout scriptures we see God unveiling Himself in diverse ways to those who sought Him diligently such as King David who described God as "The Lord is my Shepherd". Isaiah the prophet describes Him as "The Lord our Righteousness". In the assignment to bring the Israelites out of Egypt, Moses experiences him as a Deliverer through signs, wonders and miracles. When God sends His Son Jesus on the mission to save mankind, a key objective is to empower us with a name above all other names in all realms of existence. Insight into the name of Jesus is cardinal to the empowerment that comes with it.

The Apostle Paul told the Christians in Philippi - "Let this mind be in you which was also in Christ Jesus, who, being in the form of God, did not consider it robbery to be equal with God, but made Himself of no reputation, taking the form of a bondservant, and coming in the likeness of men. And being found in appearance as a man, He humbled Himself and became obedient to the point of death, even the death of the cross. Therefore, God also has highly exalted Him and given Him the name which is above every name, that at the name of Jesus every knee should bow, of those in heaven, and of those on earth, and of those under the earth, and that every tongue should confess that Jesus Christ is Lord, to the glory of God the Father" Philippians 2:5-11. In this scripture, four cardinal characteristics that culminated in the unequivocal might of the name of Jesus are Humility, Death on the Cross, Servitude and Divine Promotion.

Humility

"And being found in appearance as a man, He humbled Himself." Over the years I have noticed that the word humility is used by unbelievers and believers in a totally different context. For unbelievers it is the general sense of submission to a human order or personality while to believers it is primarily a submission to God's word and not resisting His dealings with us. There are some human traditions that are designed to humiliate certain categories or classes of people so that failure to conform to such may be considered prideful or a lack of humility. The nuance of this could be intimidating for the new Christian who as a spiritual novice may not be fully aware of the mischaracterization that could arise from conforming to God's word that may contradict human tradition. While worldly humility may guarantee our acceptance in society, spiritual humility may place us at odds with human authorities. Worldly humility is how we become yoked with the devil to fulfill his works. The Apostle Paul wrote to the Corinthians - "Do not be unequally yoked together with unbelievers. For what fellowship has righteousness with lawlessness? And what communion has light with darkness? And what accord has Christ with Belial? Or what part has a believer with an unbeliever? And what agreement has the temple of God with idols? For you are the temple of the living God. As God has said: "I will dwell in them and walk among them. I will be their God, and they shall be My people." Therefore "Come out from among them and be separate, says the Lord. Do not touch what is unclean, and I will receive you." "I will be a Father to you, and you shall be My sons and daughters, says the Lord Almighty" 2 Corinthians 6:14-18. Humility to the standards of the world yokes us with the devil. This alienates us from the life of holiness and consequently the blessings of God. Ultimately such conformity with the world is the real sense of the word pride. Jesus said – "Come to Me, all you who labor and are heavy laden, and I will give you rest. Take My yoke upon you and learn from Me, for I am gentle and lowly in heart, and you will find rest for your souls. For My yoke is easy and My burden is light" Matthew 11:28-30. Notice that Jesus requires us to become yoked to him by learning from Him. The truth makes us free from the yoke of the devil. Knowledge of truth from God's word is how we reposition ourselves to be humble before God.

Having subdued the Jewish community with their doctrines, the religious leaders were poised for political dominance assuming the Roman colonialists lost control. Since Jesus was a Jew, He represented an internal threat to their aspirations. To grasp the extent of Christ's humility, we must first imagine the glory of His majesty in heaven where He came from. He enters the human realm to poor parents and was born in a manger with animals. He was raised by a carpenter, so He had to learn one of the toughest vocations on earth. Imagine sawing wood without electric saws! He grew up in the notoriously poor town of Nazareth by which He was also identified among the Jews. Owing to all these, He was not accepted as the Messiah by the priests and the Jewish leaders of the day. He was considered a heretic.

Though He experienced constant opposition and threats from these religious leaders, Jesus demonstrated a remarkable virtue of humility. He boldly acknowledged in Matthew 5:17 - "Think not that I am come to destroy the law, or the prophets: I am not come to destroy, but to fulfill." He traveled throughout Israel preaching righteousness, encouraging the weak, demonstrating the healing power of God with miracles but then the religious leaders were blinded by their vain ambitions and publicly resisted Him. Jesus was not inhibited by their constant opposition. In spite of the resistance He experienced, Jesus did not refrain from the mission of advancing the kingdom. Humility is the virtue of overcoming personal vices, circumstantial challenges and human opposition by persisting in obedience to God's mandates. James 1:21 provides a concise definition of humility – "Wherefore lay apart all filthiness and superfluity of naughtiness, and receive with meekness the engrafted word, which is able to save your souls." Personal vices that may inhibit us include fear, arrogance and faithlessness. Circumstantial challenges may be the lack of traditional resources, tough weather conditions and demonic challenges. Human opposition may include legal restraints and competition. Humility is possible if one is able to weigh the resistance against the omnipotence of God. Ultimately God is greater than all our fears, challenges and enemies so we have no excuse to be prideful.

The Cross

"And became obedient to the point of death, even the death of the cross." The cross of Jesus Christ is symbolic of His death. His death was a sacrifice that was required of Him to redeem humanity from the wages of sin. That was a very tough call. Isaiah the prophet says of this – "Who hath believed our report? and to whom is the arm of the Lord revealed? For he shall grow up before him as a tender plant, and as a root out of a dry ground: he hath no form nor comeliness; and when we shall see him, there is no beauty that we should desire him. He is despised and rejected of men; a man of sorrows, and acquainted with grief: and we hid as it were our faces from him; he was despised, and we esteemed him not. Surely he hath borne our griefs, and carried our sorrows: yet we did esteem him stricken, smitten of God, and afflicted. But he was wounded for our transgressions, he was bruised for our iniquities: the chastisement of our peace was upon him; and with his stripes we are healed. All we like sheep have gone astray; we have turned every one to his own way; and the Lord hath laid on him the iniquity of us all" Isaiah 53:1-6. All our grief, sorrows, transgressions, iniquities, infirmities and the entire burden of humanity was placed upon Jesus at the cross of Calvary. By bearing this weight, Jesus Christ freed us from the brunt of our guilt before God. It was a cardinal part of His mission to die on the cross of Calvary and so Jesus Christ yielded to the design of God for our ultimate redemption. He did not resist the arrest of the Jewish leaders and neither did He defend Himself against all their accusations. Jesus taught the disciples that the cross was an integral part of our mission on earth.

"From that time forth began Jesus to shew unto his disciples, how that he must go unto Jerusalem, and suffer many things of the elders and chief priests and scribes, and be killed, and be raised again the third day. Then Peter took him, and began to rebuke him, saying, Be it far from thee, Lord: this shall not be unto thee. But he turned, and said unto Peter, Get thee behind me, Satan: thou art an offence unto me: for thou savourest not the things that be of God, but those that be of men. Then said Jesus unto his disciples, If any man will come after me, let him deny himself, and take up his cross, and follow me. For whosoever will save his life shall lose it: and whosoever will lose his life for my sake shall find it" Matthew 15:21-25.

Suffering of any kind is unpleasant and so it is unwelcoming to our minds as humans. Peter stood up to Jesus in protest of the doctrine of the cross. Interestingly Jesus reacts by addressing Satan as the spirit behind this protest. Obviously, Satan was going to be the principal victim of the cross so it was his inspiration that orchestrated the protest from Peter. Today there are many preachers who are peddling a gospel that brands all suffering as evidence of the abandonment or disfavor of God. This is not entirely truth for Jesus taught that the cross was not just an encounter for himself alone, but that all His followers would have to bear a cross. The cross is symbolic of self denial and death to the world. Everyone's cross is tailor made and reflects a specific area of life where God intends us to leverage unusual victory over the kingdom of darkness. Any suffering that the believer experiences by divine design is a spiritual warfare against the spirits of darkness that perpetuate such suffering against humanity. "But Judah shall dwell forever, and Jerusalem from generation to generation. For I will cleanse their blood that I have not cleansed: for the Lord dwells in Zion" Joel 3:20&21. A divine cause that is laid on us as believers is a bloodline war that must be won. The cross of each individual believer has nothing to do with the consequences for wrong choices rather it is a divine revelation enabled by the blood of Jesus. "But you have come to Mount Zion and to the city of the living God, the heavenly Jerusalem, to an innumerable company of angels, to the general assembly and church of the firstborn who are registered in heaven, to God the Judge of all, to the spirits of just men made perfect, to Jesus the Mediator of the new covenant, and to the blood of sprinkling that speaks better things than that of Abel" Hebrews 12:22-24. 'The blood of Jesus speaks better things' is a testament to how our individual burdens are unveiled. The cross assigned to each believer is an aspect of life where we must exercise apostolic mastery over the kingdom of darkness.

Until it was finally eradicated, the smallpox infection killed an estimated three hundred to five hundred million people. The solution came in 1796 when a British physician Edward Jenner came up with a method of immunization for the treatment of small pox. Here a controlled quantity of the virus is administered to the patient to impact their immune system. Immunization in most cases has helped prevent the spread of diseases such as smallpox, polio, measles, tetanus and many more. Infectious diseases act like spiritual bloodline issues. Many spiritual infirmities, issues of depravity and spiritual deprivation may be ancestral bloodline related. In such instances, God places the burden of a bloodline war on the believer and grants the grace of endurance. Like Jesus, we simply accept the conditions meted out against us by the kingdom of darkness. In the face of such challenges our attitude should be - 'Devil is this all you got?... bring it on!'

The Apostle Paul said in Romans 8:13-18, "Therefore, brethren, we are debtors, not to the flesh, to live after the flesh. For if ye live after the flesh, ye shall die: but if ye through the Spirit do mortify the deeds of the body, ye shall live. For as many as are led by the Spirit of God, they are the sons of God. For ye have not received the spirit of bondage again to fear; but ye have received the Spirit of adoption, whereby we cry, Abba, Father. The Spirit itself bears witness with our spirit, that we are the children of God: And if children, then heirs; heirs of God, and joint-heirs with Christ; if so be that we suffer with him, that we may be also glorified together. For I reckon that the sufferings of this present time are not worthy to be compared with the glory which shall be revealed in us." In any arena of life where we carry a divine burden diligently, we shall also be glorified. This means we become heavy weights in this area and may not be oppressed by the kingdom of darkness. Furthermore, in such areas of life we become intercessors for those who get challenged by the kingdom of darkness.

Servitude

"But made Himself of no reputation, taking the form of a bondservant." A servant is one who fulfills duties assigned by a master. Usually in a large estate where there are many servants, each servant or group of servants may be assigned with specific responsibilities which they execute on a regular basis. Such is the picture of our world where God is the master and all of us humans are servants with assigned responsibilities. While on earth Jesus relinquished the master-status of His divinity and assumed the human-status of a servant. "How God anointed Jesus of Nazareth with the Holy Ghost and with power: who went about doing good, and healing all that were oppressed of the devil; for God was with him" Acts 10:38. Notice, the purpose of the anointing upon Jesus was to facilitate His mission. In the same way, God anoints us so we can be effective servants. You will notice also that the ministry of Jesus is profound and impactful to us humans. He went about doing good and healing all who were oppressed by the devil in a working relationship with God. In the same way God worked with Adam in the function of naming God's works, Jesus had a working relationship with God in servitude. Today the word servant is sometimes viewed as meaning slavery, so many people shy away from identifying with this word. In some extreme cases people do not want to function in the framework of a master-servant relationship. The practice of slavery as we know it from recent history is a perverted form of servitude where slave owners grossly abused their slaves. African-Americans who were brought into North America in slave ships experienced the horrors of inhumane treatment by their slave masters for several years. Today however many of the abuses of the master-servant relationship have been addressed through labor laws that guide employers and their employees. Such labor laws for fair practice in employer and employee relationships were given to Moses and enshrined in the scriptures, but then ignorance of the scriptures is the reason that slavery still exists in certain sectors of society.

Fundamentally, a servant is one who identifies their calling or the anointing and works to fulfill their assignment in a working relationship with God. Servitude is how we are privileged to impact our generation with our divine endowments. While our service may fall within the framework of an existing institution with a hierarchy of leadership, it does not diminish the essence of the God-factor. As an example to us, Jesus was trained and served in the vocation of Joseph who was His earthly custodian. Servitude is not a terrible status to be frowned at, rather it is the pathway for impacting our world with the divine endowments that are inherent within us. Ambition is the opposite of servitude. A classic example is the generation following Noah and his sons. "Now the whole earth had one language and one speech. And it came to pass, as they journeyed from the east, that they found a plain in the land of Shinar, and they dwelt there. Then they said to one another, "Come, let us make bricks and bake them thoroughly." They had brick for stone, and they had asphalt for mortar. And they said, "Come, let us build ourselves a city, and a tower whose top is in the heavens; let us make a name for ourselves, lest we be scattered abroad over the face of the whole earth." But the Lord came down to see the city and the tower which the sons of men had built. And the Lord said, "Indeed the people are one and they all have one language, and this is what they begin to do; now nothing that they propose to do will be withheld from them. Come, let Us go down and there confuse their language, that they may not understand one another's speech." So the Lord scattered them abroad from there over the face of all the earth, and they ceased building the city. Therefore its name is called Babel, because there the Lord confused the language of all the earth; and from there the Lord scattered them abroad over the face of all the earth" Genesis 11:1-9.

Notice the ambition of these people to build a city and make themselves a name. Their ultimate goal was to defy the plans of God for them to fill the earth. The usage of the word 'ambition' is traced to the Roman era when politicians who were running for a seat in the Senate would go around seeking for votes. Ambition is associated with the quest for political power. As in the case of the tower of Babel, ambition that defies God's plan for our lives invokes the judgment of God. The pursuit of purpose is God's design that draws us into a working relationship through the anointing resident in us.

Promotion

"Therefore God also has highly exalted Him and given Him the name which is above every name, that at the name of Jesus every knee should bow, of those in heaven, and of those on earth, and of those under the earth, and that every tongue should confess that Jesus Christ is Lord, to the glory of God the Father."

Today, Americans are highly obsessed with the notion of human stardom. People literally idolize those who have become proclaimed stars. While these may be individuals who have distinguished themselves in a vocation, entertainment or sports discipline and may genuinely inspire creativity and excellence, the sheer obsession with such so-called stars is quite abominable. For instance, the entertainment and media industries have crafted ways for elevating people to stardom status. However, the unusually heavy scheduling pressure associated with such stardom has resulted in chronic drug abuse and consequent premature death of those who could not handle the stress of it all. One of my mentors, Rev. Andrew Asare taught me about the various kinds of promotion: Self-Promotion, Satan's Promotion and God's Promotion.

Self-Promotion is to devise a means to endorse oneself above others. There are several ways to attain self-promotion. In the past those who aspired to be kings or national leaders waged a coup and murdered the reigning ruler. Today if you are part of an institution, you may employ character assassination to discredit and eliminate those who are legitimately ahead of you in the leadership hierarchy. People steal the intellectual property of others to start their own enterprises. If you can afford the means to advertise, it is possible to promote oneself through the channels of the mass media. Unfortunately, American society does not frown on self-promotion so it has become a norm.

Satan's Promotion is any form of popularity that is demonic inspired. We identify demonic inspiration by the impact of merchandise. Does the rise to fame of a person promote moral decadence? If so, then it is inspired by the kingdom of darkness. In America today, there are famous musicians who propagate a culture of hate through the lyrics of their music, talk shows that promote moral vices and many movies that promote moral perversions to desensitize society from shunning such practices. Yet those who are champions of such are the stars of society and often dictate the trends of American culture.

God's Promotion is the legitimate ascension to prominence and leadership. "I said unto the fools, Deal not foolishly: and to the wicked, Lift not up the horn: Lift not up your horn on high: speak not with a stiff neck. For promotion cometh neither from the east, nor from the west, nor from the south. But God is the judge: he putteth down one, and setteth up another. For in the hand of the Lord there is a cup, and the wine is red; it is full of mixture; and he poureth out of the same: but the dregs thereof, all the wicked of the earth shall wring them out, and drink them. But I will declare for ever; I will sing praises to the God of Jacob. All the horns of the wicked also will I cut off; but the horns of the righteous shall be exalted" Psalm 75:4-10.

Throughout history we learn of those who found a way to bump themselves into fame and leadership but ended up shamefully abased. The fact here is that God is the one who elevates to prominence and leadership. He sets down and lifts up as a function of His Sovereignty. Jesus Christ was highly exalted by God and given a name above all other names in heaven, on earth and under the earth. I have personally experienced the power in the name of Jesus Christ as I invoked this name while in prayer for victims of demonic oppression. I have witnessed instant deliverance from oppression and healing from infirmities in the name of Jesus Christ. The power in the name of Jesus is very real and has not diminished ever since the victory at the cross of Calvary. The Apostles of Jesus invoked the name of Jesus Christ for notable signs, wonders and miracles at the onset of the New Testament Church. It was the selling point for the gospel of salvation and would always remain the victory of the believer over the forces of darkness and human oppression. "And God wrought special miracles by the hands of Paul: So that from his body were brought unto the sick handkerchiefs or aprons, and the diseases departed from them, and the evil spirits went out of them. Then certain of the vagabond Jews, exorcists, took upon them to call over them which had evil spirits the name of the Lord Jesus, saying, We adjure you by Jesus whom Paul preacheth. And there were seven sons of one Sceva, a Jew, and chief of the priests, which did so. And the evil spirit answered and said, Jesus I know, and Paul I know; but who are ye? And the man in whom the evil spirit was leaped on them, and overcame them, and prevailed against them, so that they fled out of that house naked and wounded. And this was known to all the Jews and Greeks also dwelling at Ephesus; and fear fell on them all, and the name of the Lord Jesus was magnified" Acts 19:11-17.

Where there is divine promotion, the influence is not just in the realm of humanity but transcends into the demonic realm. Demons stay away and bow to whoever God has exalted over them.

In the same way God exalted the name of Jesus as reward for his humility, sacrifice at the cross and servitude of mankind God's promotion is the reward for faithfulness. "He that is faithful in that which is least is faithful also in much: and he that is unjust in the least is unjust also in much. If therefore ye have not been faithful in the unrighteous mammon, who will commit to your trust the true riches? And if ye have not been faithful in that which is another man's, who shall give you that which is your own? No servant can serve two masters: for either he will hate the one, and love the other; or else he will hold to the one, and despise the other. Ye cannot serve God and mammon. And the Pharisees also, who were covetous, heard all these things: and they derided him. And he said unto them, Ye are they which justify yourselves before men; but God knoweth your hearts: for that which is highly esteemed among men is abomination in the sight of God" Luke 16:10-15.

It is interesting that the Pharisees derided Jesus after hearing the fundamental premise for divine promotion. The Pharisees already had a system in place by which they promoted those within their ranks and this method precluded faithfulness. Jesus described such human promotion as an abomination in the sight of God. Faithfulness is a virtue that consists of humility to God, death to self and servitude in the arena of our anointing. When we are faithful to God, He opens doors before us to rise from one level of influence to another. As we prove faithful at a level of servitude, we justify our capacity for increase in responsibility. As our responsibilities are increased so does our range of influence. We must never seek to make a name for ourselves because fame is a natural consequence within our sphere of influence. Genuine fame is simply the testimony of our faithful impact.

4

The Culture of Encounter

*"Remember the Sabbath day, to keep it holy. Six days you
shall labor and do all your work, but the seventh day is the
Sabbath of the Lord your God. In it you shall do no work: you,
nor your son, nor your daughter, nor your male servant, nor
your female servant, nor your cattle, nor your stranger
who is within your gates. For in six days the Lord made the
heavens and the earth, the sea, and all that is in them, and
rested the seventh day. Therefore the Lord blessed
the Sabbath day and hallowed it"*
Exodus 20:8-11

On a Sunday morning several years ago, I was in
Dallas and decided to fellowship at the Potters House.
While driving on the freeway that morning from
Carrolton there was heavy traffic and I said to myself,
'Wow, so much people, heading to Church'. At the
point where the traffic subsided, I realized it was an

exit leading to a stadium where fans were gathering for a game that was billed for later in the afternoon. I was baffled and felt such disappointment because my impression of the Bible-belt area was that a huge chunk of the population was inclined to attend Church on a typical Sunday morning. Today, many Christians would easily choose a sporting activity or entertainment event over a Church event. It is a cultural shift that is not only precarious but responsible for some of the deepest crisis in America today. It is no secret that many Americans are struggling in life, sickly, saddled with debt and have near zero-equity. Interestingly, the Sabbath day rule which is the fourth of the Ten Commandments was the short version of several Sabbath-oriented instructions that mitigate these challenges. These instructions were divinely designed to foster rest from our struggles, redemption from bondage, release from debt and restoration from disinheritance. The Sabbath signifies divine appointments that acted like a pendulum oscillating through time to foster change in human conditions of derangement.

There was a Weekly Sabbath, Annual Sabbath, Seventh-year Sabbath and the Fiftieth-year Sabbath. God weaved the Sabbath into the sequence of creation as a breaking point for potential manifestations of evil so that we would not become trapped with endless struggle, bondage, debt and disinheritance. Like the Jews of the Old Testament days, we have misconstrued the revelation of the Sabbath, succumbing to it as though a religious ritual and missed the essence of divine encounters.

Rest from Struggle

"And on the seventh day God ended His work which He had done, and He rested on the seventh day from all His work which He had done. Then God blessed the seventh day and sanctified it, because in it He rested from all His work which God had created and made." Genesis 2:2&3

For approximately 2,500 years after God observed the first Sabbath, He continued faithfully and never required man to observe it until He was ready to establish Israel as a nation. There are two things God did on the Sabbath – 'Sanctified' and 'Blessed'. 'Sanctified' means to be cleansed. 'Blessed' means that God released words that activates His angels to foster goodness. The Sabbath is a divine encounter where we are cleansed from all that desecrates us so that we can experience God's goodness. It is interesting that many of the recorded miracles that Jesus did during

71

His life here on earth occurred on the Sabbath. A classic example is the healing at the pool of Bethesda:

"After this there was a feast of the Jews, and Jesus went up to Jerusalem. Now there is in Jerusalem by the Sheep Gate a pool, which is called in Hebrew, Bethesda, having five porches. In these lay a great multitude of sick people, blind, lame, paralyzed, waiting for the moving of the water. For an angel went down at a certain time into the pool and stirred up the water; then whoever stepped in first, after the stirring of the water, was made well of whatever disease he had. Now a certain man was there who had an infirmity thirty-eight years. When Jesus saw him lying there, and knew that he already had been in that condition a long time, He said to him, "Do you want to be made well?" The sick man answered Him, "Sir, I have no man to put me into the pool when the water is stirred up; but while I am coming, another steps down before me." Jesus said to him, "Rise, take up your bed and walk." And immediately the man was made well, took up his bed, and walked. And that day was the Sabbath. The Jews therefore said to him who was cured, "It is the Sabbath; it is not lawful for you to carry your bed." He answered them, "He who made me well said to me, 'Take up your bed and walk.'" Then they asked him, "Who is the Man who said to you, 'Take up your bed and walk'?" But the one who was healed did not know who it was, for Jesus had withdrawn, a multitude being in that place. Afterward Jesus found him in the temple, and said to him, "See, you have been made well. Sin no more, lest a worse thing come upon you." The man departed and told the Jews that it was Jesus who had made him well. For this reason the Jews persecuted Jesus, and sought to kill Him, because He had done these things on the Sabbath. But Jesus answered them, "My Father has been working until now, and I have been working" John 5:1-17

Notice that it was during a feast that an angel would stir the pool of Bethesda. The first person to jump into the pool after it had been stirred by the angel got healed. Unfortunately for this individual in the story, he never had help to out-jump the others when the pool was stirred by the angel. Jesus came to the pool on the Sabbath day of a feast to heal this man who had been lame thirty-eight years. He told the lame man 'Rise, take up your bed and walk'. The religious leaders were at constant variance with Jesus, persecuted and even plotted to kill him for this. Clearly these religious leaders were more concerned that people observe the various rules they had established for Sabbath-compliance. They monitored the people closely looking for violators to punish. The Sabbath was the day of religious prominence for these Jewish leaders. They were not interested in the miracle healing of the Sabbath rather they sought an opportunity to terminate the ministry of Jesus to the people. As in the days of Jesus' earthly ministry, today, both clergy and laity have missed the concept of the Sabbath completely. Church leaders are more interested in the number count of those who attend services because it guarantees increased offerings and the significance of prominence. As a result, Church leaders are constantly looking for crafty ways to increase the size of the congregation. Some of the methods that are being employed for Church growth are anti-scriptures and just ludicrous. Similarly today, many attend Church services because they want to be in the good books of God. How sad! They do not want to incite the disfavor of God and lose their job, their spouse, children to drugs, their health and well-being. It sounds as though people have been manipulated to think that being religious is a way to pacify the heart of an angry God!

Jesus put the Sabbath in perspective – "And He said to them, "The Sabbath was made for man, and not man for the Sabbath. Therefore the Son of Man is also Lord of the Sabbath" Mark 2:27&28. The Sabbath is an appointed time for divine visitation to break the manifestations of evil in society. If the Jewish leaders had the Sabbath in true perspective they would have embraced the ministry of Jesus to the people. Today if we would embrace the revelation of the Sabbath as an appointed time for divine encounter, I believe that every Sabbath we shall be cleansed from all that contaminates our spirit and receive the goodness of God that is unveiled on these occasions. Psalm 107:20 says "He sent His word and healed them, and delivered them from their destructions."

It is no doubt that life on planet earth tends to be a struggle for most people. The necessities of life get complicated more and more with the advancement of civilization and technology. Those who are not from financially rich backgrounds and not privileged to afford college education or employment in high paying jobs most often find themselves on the borderline of crisis. Poverty, debt, joblessness, homelessness, family dysfunction, divorce, sickness and disease are among the many challenges that most people grapple with on a daily basis. At every point in time, these issues come and go like clockwork in a never-ending cycle.

In the scheme of God's creation, there is a place for light as well as darkness. This means that there is a provision of good from the light to overcome the challenges of evil from the darkness. The light of God is His design to bring us into His rest after every six days. "Let us therefore be diligent to enter that rest, lest anyone fall according to the same example of disobedience. For the word of God is living and powerful, and sharper than any two-edged sword, piercing even to the division of soul and spirit, and of joints and marrow, and is a discerner of the thoughts and intents of the heart" Hebrews 4:11&12. Every week God furnishes us with His word through His ministers. His word facilitates us to overcome the challenges for the coming week. God's omnipotent abilities are enshrined in His word. As the sharpest double-edged sword, it equips us to defeat all the schemes of darkness that are against us. As a double-edged sword, God's word convicts us to overcome psychological inhibitions and also to make godly decisions. "For this is the love of God, that we keep His commandments. And His commandments are not burdensome. For whatever is born of God overcomes the world. And this is the victory that has overcome the world—our faith" 1 John 5:3&4.

With the ceaseless bombardment of evil that confront us, it is easy to assume that God may have abandoned us in this world. I have heard people say this, "If God is still in control, then why is there so much evil in society?" On the first day of creation we know that 'Day and Night' were parts of His divine design so 'Good and Evil' co-exists. The ability to overcome evil is enshrined in God's word that activates our faith. Our victory enablement is in our faith. "So then faith comes by hearing, and hearing by the word of God" Romans 10:17. We have to hear God's word by the mouth of His Ministers whom He sends to enable our faith. Faith triggers a reaction of our hearts towards the challenges that confront us. It anchors our soul to God who gives us victory and solutions.

"Now faith is the substance of things hoped for, the evidence of things not seen. For by it the elders obtained a good testimony. By faith we understand that the worlds were framed by the word of God, so that the things which are seen were not made of things which are visible" Hebrews 11:1-3.

Faith is a spiritual substance that embodies the victory and solutions that we seek from God. It comes as a revelation of truth that we must believe. This truth may require some form of obedience on our part to certain commandments. When we have done due diligence of obedience, faith requires us to hope in God until the victory or solution manifests. In the book of Hebrews, the scripture accounts for those who hinged their lives upon faith in God. "And what more shall I say? For the time would fail me to tell of Gideon and Barak and Samson and Jephthah, also of David and Samuel and the prophets: who through faith subdued kingdoms, worked righteousness, obtained promises, stopped the mouths of lions, quenched the violence of fire, escaped the edge of the sword, out of weakness were made strong, became valiant in battle, turned to flight the armies of the aliens. Women received their dead raised to life again. Others were tortured, not accepting deliverance, that they might obtain a better resurrection. Still others had trial of mockings and scourgings, yes, and of chains and imprisonment. They were stoned, they were sawn in two, were tempted, were slain with the sword. They wandered about in sheepskins and goatskins, being destitute, afflicted, tormented— of whom the world was not worthy. They wandered in deserts and mountains, in dens and caves of the earth. And all these, having obtained a good testimony through faith, did not receive the promise, God having provided something better for us, that they should not be made perfect apart from us" Hebrews 11:32-40.

Faith is the testimony of how God's works are demonstrated through all those who walk with Him from generation to generation. It is a story that started from Adam, through Abel, Seth and the Enoch, Noah, Abraham, Isaac, Jacob, Joseph, Moses, Joshua and all those who walked with God faithfully as scripture tells us. In recent years we are aware of the fruits born by Ministers of God who fostered the Great Awakenings in America such as D.L. Moody, Charles Finney, Alexander Dowie, Aimee Semple-Mcpherson, Jack Coe, John G. Lake, Oral Roberts and many more. Week after week we are furnished with renewed mandates in the different areas of life where we may be under siege of the kingdom of darkness. We can only know those fresh mandates when we attend services where God's ministers are positioned as conduits for streaming the word of our faith. Sabbath mandates are our key to uprightness. "...just as Christ also loved the church and gave Himself for her, that He might sanctify and cleanse her with the washing of water by the word, that He might present her to Himself a glorious church, not having spot or wrinkle or any such thing, but that she should be holy and without blemish" Ephesians 5:25b-27. Spots, wrinkles and blemishes rob us of our uprightness. In every aspect of life where we are saddled with spots, wrinkles and blemishes our authority over the enemy is diminished considerably. "Therefore the Lord has recompensed me according to my righteousness, According to the cleanness of my hands in His sight. With the merciful You will show Yourself merciful; With a blameless man You will show Yourself blameless; With the pure You will show Yourself pure; And with the devious You will show Yourself shrewd. For You will save the humble people, But will bring down haughty looks" Psalm 18:24-27. As it clearly denotes, uprightness is to stand straight with God. Imagine how frustrating it will be to stand at an angle sideways and attempt to shoot an arrow! Alignment with God's word positions us to stand straight and launch with divine power against the enemy of our rest in God.

Redemption from Bondage

Certain areas of life where we continue to experience challenges week after week though we are exercising the fullness of our faith may have the resemblance of demonic bondage. Usually these are areas of our lives that were subjected to ancestral covenants. Out of desperation and ignorance our ancestors may have sought help from witch doctors, clairvoyants or diviners who invoked demonic spirits. The devil does not love anyone, so he provides 'temporary relief' to the desperate based upon his conditions. Most often there is a negotiation where territories are exchanged. For instance, the demon of sickness troubling a person trades places with the demon of poverty. This means that a demonic relationship is established and the person who was previously oppressed by sickness is now oppressed by poverty. The bloodlines of those who seek help from the demonic world become enslaved by demonic spirits. A believer who is a victim of demonic bondage can only be redeemed by the blood of Jesus. The blood of Jesus Christ has to be invoked to break the demonic covenant responsible for the bondage. Some chronic infirmities and psychological issues may be associated with demonic oppression. The Passover Feast initiated the final plague that made the Pharaoh of Egypt set the Israelites free from bondage in Egypt. This bondage may have been established by the blood covenant that came into effect when Abraham and Hagar the Egyptian conceived Ishmael. God instructed the Israelites to commemorate the Passover annually so that He will revisit them to ensure their continual redemption. During the season of Passover was when Jesus Christ was crucified and shed His blood at Calvary for our redemption. Jesus told the disciples to always celebrate His death through the administration of communion. The annual feasts of Israel were divinely appointed times for God's visitation where various manifestations of bondage were broken. Here is a list of such annual feasts and the evils associated with them:

1. Passover – Spiritual, Emotional and Physical Bondage
2. First-fruits (Resurrection) – Corruption, Weakness, Carnality and Dishonor
3. Pentecost – Poverty
4. Trumpets – Disorderliness
5. Atonement – Injustice
6. Tabernacles – Disinheritance

If we observe these feasts as we should, the power of God is manifested through the cross of our Lord Jesus Christ to deliver us from all forms of demonic oppression. Every year as we honor the appointed times, we receive a divine encounter of deliverance from demonic oppression. God's word enshrines the capacity to heal and deliver from every condition orchestrated by the kingdom of darkness. It is the basis of our faith and mandate for prayer and deliverance. God's word is our authority to bind the forces of demonic oppression as well as loosen the good things of life.

Release from Debt

Every human being has an obligation to society. We are all uniquely endowed with potentials to serve for the good of our generation. Failure to administer our potentials to make an impact is the principal debt. Elisha's solution to a widow in debt unveils this truth.

"A certain woman of the wives of the sons of the prophets cried out to Elisha, saying, "Your servant my husband is dead, and you know that your servant feared the Lord. And the creditor is coming to take my two sons to be his slaves." So Elisha said to her, "What shall I do for you? Tell me, what do you have in the house?" And she said, "Your maidservant has nothing in the house but a jar of oil." Then he said,

"Go, borrow vessels from everywhere, from all your
neighbors—empty vessels; do not gather just a
few. And when you have come in, you shall shut the
door behind you and your sons; then pour it into all
those vessels, and set aside the full ones." So she
went from him and shut the door behind her and her
sons, who brought the vessels to her; and she
poured it out. Now it came to pass, when the vessels
were full, that she said to her son, "Bring me another
vessel." And he said to her, "There is not another
vessel." So the oil ceased. Then she came and told the
man of God. And he said, "Go, sell the oil and pay
your debt; and you and your sons live on the rest" 2
King 4:1-7.

It is clear from this story that the widow's
indebtedness was a condition created by the failure to
impact her neighbors with her oil. As we have learnt
earlier, the oil signifies the anointing. Though the jar
of oil was her only resource, it had the potential to
impact her neighbors and hence change her condition
of indebtedness. The anointing is the endowment of
God that enables us to manifest unique abilities.
Failure to function in the anointing is like an
important part of a machine that malfunctions. This
may render the entire machine useless until that part
starts to function again. We are all part of the machine
of God to foster the progress of our world and so
failure to function is a core debt. Within His calendar

83

for mankind is a schedule that gives everyone an opportunity out of indebtedness.

"At the end of every seven years you shall grant a release of debts. And this is the form of the release: Every creditor who has lent anything to his neighbor shall release it; he shall not require it of his neighbor or his brother, because it is called the Lord's release. Of a foreigner you may require it; but you shall give up your claim to what is owed by your brother, except when there may be no poor among you; for the Lord will greatly bless you in the land which the Lord your God is giving you to possess as an inheritance— only if you carefully obey the voice of the Lord your God, to observe with care all these commandments which I command you today. For the Lord your God will bless you just as He promised you; you shall lend to many nations, but you shall not borrow; you shall reign over many nations, but they shall not reign over you. "If there is among you a poor man of your brethren, within any of the gates in your land which the Lord your God is giving you, you shall not harden your heart nor shut your hand from your poor brother, but you shall open your hand wide to him and willingly lend him sufficient for his need, whatever he needs. Beware lest there be a wicked thought in your heart, saying, 'The seventh year, the year of release, is at hand,' and your eye be evil against your poor brother and you give him nothing, and he cry out to the Lord against you, and it become sin among you. You shall surely give to him, and your heart should not be grieved when you give to him, because for this thing the Lord your God will bless you in all your works and in all to which you put your hand. For the poor will never cease from the land; therefore I command you, saying, 'You shall open your hand wide to your brother, to your poor and your needy, in your land.' "If your brother, a Hebrew man, or a Hebrew woman, is sold to you and serves you six years, then in the seventh year you shall let him go free from you. And when you send him away free from you, you shall not let him go away empty-handed; you shall supply him liberally from your flock, from your threshing floor, and from your winepress. From what the Lord your God has blessed you with, you shall give to him. You shall remember that you were a slave in the land of Egypt, and the Lord your God redeemed you; therefore I command you this thing today" Deuteronomy 15:1-15.

In God's calendar, after every six years, the seventh year was declared a year of 'Release'. The Release required God's people to observe the following: First, everyone was to release their fellow Israelites from the debts they owed. Second, they must freely give to meet the needs of the poor. Third, they must release those who were in bond-service as a result of their debts. Fourth, those who were released from bond-service should be furnished with resources to jumpstart their lives. Fifth, those who offered to be bond-servants were to be allowed to serve in their calling of purpose.

Ultimately the release was designed to give everyone in society an opportunity to bounce back from indebtedness. God promised to elevate everyone who practiced the release – "For the Lord your God will bless you just as He promised you; you shall lend to many nations, but you shall not borrow; you shall reign over many nations, but they shall not reign over you." Elisha counseled the widow to borrow not a few vessels from her neighbors. This means that we must not limit the scope of our impact. The widow's oil run out when the last borrowed vessel was filled. Our oil is not limited but a limited vision is the limitation of our impact.

Restoration from Disinheritance

Home ownership in most cases is a twenty-five year journey that everyone with a mortgage looks forward to complete. Investment into home ownership is the fundamental way ordinary people build equity and so a loss of one's home can be very disheartening.

Through the unscrupulous deals of mortgage bankers and some Wall Street investment brokers, there was an economic meltdown in 2007 that was responsible for the loss of many homes and investments in the US. It came to light that amidst all the dubious schemes, financial institutions concocted schemes and forged documents to repossess the properties of ordinary people all across the country. Many big corporations and institutions engage the services of lobbyists who influence legislation in Washington DC so that whenever a scheme for defrauding Americans is unraveled, they quickly come up with new schemes hidden and enshrined in new legislations. In every election cycle we find the promise of solutions by politicians as a vague appeasement to the human sentiment. God alone holds the key to our restoration and His calendar incorporated provisions for restoration from disinheritance.

"And you shall count seven Sabbaths of years for yourself, seven times seven years; and the time of the seven Sabbaths of years shall be to you forty-nine years. Then you shall cause the trumpet of the Jubilee to sound on the tenth day of the seventh month; on the Day of Atonement you shall make the trumpet to sound throughout all your land. And you shall consecrate the fiftieth year, and proclaim liberty throughout all the land to all its inhabitants. It shall be a Jubilee for you; and each of you shall return to his possession, and each of you shall return to his family. That fiftieth year shall be a Jubilee to you; in it you shall neither sow nor reap what grows of its own accord, nor gather the grapes of your untended vine. For it is the Jubilee; it shall be holy to you; you shall eat its produce from the field. 'In this Year of Jubilee, each of you shall return to his possession. And if you sell anything to your neighbor or buy from your neighbor's hand, you shall not oppress one another. According to the number of years after the Jubilee you shall buy from your neighbor, and according to the number of years of crops he shall sell to you. According to the multitude of years you shall increase its price, and according to the fewer number of years you shall diminish its price; for he sells to you according to the number of the years of the crops. Therefore you shall not oppress one another, but you shall fear your God; for I am the Lord your God" Leviticus 25:8-17.

The Jubilee was a divine provision for restoration of God's people from disinheritance. Every fifty years the trumpet of the Jubilee was sounded so every Israelite would return to their original heritage of family and land. God required that all transactions of real estate revolve around the Jubilee because He did not design for anyone to be permanently disinherited. Technically, lands outside city walls were to be leased and not sold. The value of the lease would be estimated around the next Jubilee. Assuming there were five years to the Jubilee, the land could only be leased for five years because in the year of the Jubilee all leased lands reverted to the original owners.

Restoration is the divine way by which God enables us gain and keep our inheritance in Christ. "And I will restore to you the years that the locust hath eaten, the cankerworm, and the caterpillar, and the palmerworm, my great army which I sent among you. And ye shall eat in plenty, and be satisfied, and praise the name of the Lord your God, that hath dealt wondrously with you: and my people shall never be ashamed" Joel 2:25&26. The locust, cankerworm, caterpillar and palmerworm are symbolic of the systemic ways by which we are disinherited. Restoration starts with a divine promise. Whenever God makes a promise of an inheritance, it is a covenant proposal. When He reveals what He would accomplish in our lives, it is equally important that we find out our role to play. A covenant requires consideration for both parties. This means that all parties to a covenant must play at least a token role to keep the covenant valid.

"For I am the Lord, I do not change; Therefore you are not consumed, O sons of Jacob. Yet from the days of your fathers, You have gone away from My ordinances, And have not kept them. Return to Me, and I will return to you," Says the Lord of hosts. "But you said, 'In what way shall we return?' "Will a man rob God? Yet you have robbed Me! But you say, 'In what way have we robbed You?' In tithes and offerings. You are cursed with a curse, For you have robbed Me, Even this whole nation. Bring all the tithes into the storehouse, That there may be food in My house, And try Me now in this," Says the Lord of hosts, "If I will not open for you the windows of heaven, And pour out for you such blessing, That there will not be room enough to receive it. "And I will rebuke the devourer for your sakes, So that he will not destroy the fruit of your ground, Nor shall the vine fail to bear fruit for you in the field," Says the Lord of hosts; "And all nations will call you blessed, For you will be a delightful land," Says the Lord of hosts" Malachi 3:6-12.

Notice that this scripture reveals the consequence of a broken covenant in tithing. It gives the devourer access to rob God's people. However, God is willing to return to the covenant and protect our blessings if only we return to faithfulness in tithing. The story in the book of Ruth about the family of Elimelech with his wife Naomi and their two sons Malon and Chilon underscores the premise of return. During a famine in Bethlehem-Judah where they lived originally, they liquidated their assets and migrated to Moab a heathen nation. Mahlon and Chilion take up Moabite wives by the names Orpah and Ruth. Elimelech, Mahlon and Chilion died in Moab and were survived by their wives Naomi, Orpah and Ruth. Naomi heard that God had visited Bethlehem-Judah with bread so she returned with Ruth. Though they came back disinherited, through the divine provision of gleaning and kinsman redemption by their relative Boaz, the scripture shows that Naomi and Ruth gained back their inheritance.

5

The Culture of Honor

*"Honor your father and your mother, that your days may be
long upon the land which the Lord your God is giving you"*
Exodus 20:12

Recently I had an interesting conversation with a
retired teacher in his seventies. He asked not to be
mentioned by name, so I will refer to him as Jack. He
seemed deeply concerned about the cultural
breakdown of the American society and the family
dysfunction. Jack lamented that disrespect for the
elderly is a cancer in society and that unfortunately
there was too little in the school system that addresses
the virtue of honor. As a teacher in a depraved
neighborhood, he always had to establish the premise
for honor with his students at the beginning of the
school term in order to maintain order. It worked! He
told of how the cars of his fellow teachers would be

93

ransacked by the unruly students and yet his car was never touched. The students respected him because he established the premise of honor. He retired prematurely because at some point fellow teachers developed an attitude of 'you don't bother me, you pass to the next grade!!!' Students were being promoted not based on merit but as a 'survival mode' for teachers. Jack mentioned the breakdown in the family structure as also key to dishonor in society. The explosive increase of the single parent syndrome with the consequent socio-economic challenges that prevent families seating down at the dinner table together to share meals and exchange ideas. He laments that because of the abandonment of the values that kept families together many young people in society today cannot grasp the concept that the elder is chief in society.

A father and mother are leaders of the family unit. The first institution established by God was marriage in the Garden of Eden. Adam and Eve were the first human leaders in the history of this world. The fifth commandment is a fundamental leadership rule that assigns honor for all who lead human institutions. Honor means dignity and respect. While dignity means self-worth, respect is to pay due attention and refrain from violating those in authority. Honor enshrines decent character and adherence to standards and values. Though many in society today consider only the monetary calculation of net worth as the value of a man, the level of honor in a human being is their real worth. For every child who aspires to be a parent; a protégé that hopes to be a mentor or follower who desires to become a leader, honor is the future-status-domicile. The promise of long life to those who honor parents is testament to a future-status-domicile. In other words, if you honor leaders, there is a place of leadership for you to occupy in the future.

There was an interesting confrontation on this subject between Jesus and the religious leaders of the day. "Then the scribes and Pharisees who were from Jerusalem came to Jesus, saying, "Why do Your disciples transgress the tradition of the elders? For they do not wash their hands when they eat bread." He answered and said to them, "Why do you also transgress the commandment of God because of your tradition? For God commanded, saying, 'Honor your father and your mother'; and, 'He who curses father or mother, let him be put to death.' But you say, 'Whoever says to his father or mother, "Whatever profit you might have received from me is a gift to God"— then he need not honor his father or mother.' Thus you have made the commandment of God of no effect by your tradition. Hypocrites! Well did Isaiah prophesy about you, saying: 'These people draw near to Me with their mouth, And honor Me with their lips, But their heart is far from Me. And in vain they worship Me, Teaching as doctrines the commandments of men.' When He had called the multitude to Himself, He said to them, "Hear and understand: Not what goes into the mouth defiles a man; but what comes out of the mouth, this defiles a man" Matthew 15:1-11.

The religious leaders were offended that the disciples of Jesus ate without first washing their hands. This was one of several doctrines they had coined for their fellow Jews and demanded compliance. Jesus cut through their crap of hypocrisy by addressing the 'so called' doctrines that were a deviation from God's true commandments. Any tradition that fundamentally departs from the truth of God's word is not an acceptable heritage. Secondly, the religious leaders neutralized the commandment to honor father and mother by suggesting that parents should not expect their children to be responsible and invest in the family legacy. They contend that parents should consider any help from their children as a gift and not an obligation of honor. Jesus remarked that these religious leaders were hypocrites in their ways – "Teaching as doctrines the commandments of men." They crafted rules and regulations that suited their agenda to lord it over their fellow Jews and yet not to be accountable themselves.

Honor primarily enshrines accountability to God's word. "Let every soul be subject to the governing authorities. For there is no authority except from

God, and the authorities that exist are appointed by God. Therefore whoever resists the authority resists the ordinance of God, and those who resist will bring judgment on themselves. For rulers are not a terror to good works, but to evil. Do you want to be unafraid of the authority? Do what is good, and you will have praise from the same. For he is God's minister to you for good. But if you do evil, be afraid; for he does not bear the sword in vain; for he is God's minister, an avenger to execute wrath on him who practices evil. Therefore you must be subject, not only because of wrath but also for conscience' sake. For because of this you also pay taxes, for they are God's ministers attending continually to this very thing. Render therefore to all their due: taxes to whom taxes are due, customs to whom customs, fear to whom fear, honor to whom honor" Romans 13:1-7.

Leaders are ministers of God that administer the affairs of mankind. They deserve our respect. Ideally human leaders mimic God's role in our lives in a measured instance. Their role is to establish the framework of relevant rules, discipline, posterity and legacy that ultimately bring benefits of progress to all.

Heritage

The first premise of honor is heritage. The dictionary defines heritage as values handed down from previous generations. God used the potential of heritage as the premise for choosing Abraham's lineage as a channel of blessing to mankind. "And the Lord said, "Shall I hide from Abraham what I am doing, since Abraham shall surely become a great and mighty nation, and all the nations of the earth shall be blessed in him? For I have known him, in order that he may command his children and his household after him, that they keep the way of the Lord, to do righteousness and justice, that the Lord may bring to Abraham what He has spoken to him" Genesis 18:17-19. Abraham had the unique quality of training those of his household with his skills and values. In the instance of the kings who had defeated Sodom and captured his nephew Lot, Abraham went after them with 318 servants trained in his house to recover Lot. Abraham passed on whatever God taught him to Isaac, and Isaac passed these on to Jacob so that this lineage kept building up a heritage of divine values. Neglect of heritage is a core reason for which Esau lost the blessings of Abraham to his brother Jacob. With the buildup of divine values in Joseph, he was able to administer the affairs of Egypt and saved the nation from the consequences of a seven-year drought. Moses eventually penned down the history of the world up to his time by tapping into divine revelation and oral tradition. Today we have the scriptures that holy men of God were inspired to record for our learning. As believers we are saved through Jesus Christ into the heritage of Abraham. "That the blessing of Abraham might come upon the Gentiles in Christ Jesus, that we might receive the promise of the Spirit through faith" Galatians 3:14. The patriarchs who modeled divine values, set for us a standard that defines our culture as Christians. Jesus Christ invoked the scriptures to articulate the gospel and demonstrated how we overcome the world by faith. The Apostle Paul admonishes his protégé Timothy - "But you have carefully followed my doctrine, manner of life, purpose, faith, longsuffering, love, perseverance, persecutions, afflictions, which happened to me at Antioch, at Iconium, at Lystra— what persecutions I endured. And out of them all the Lord delivered me. Yes, and all who desire to live godly in Christ Jesus will suffer persecution. But evil men and impostors will grow worse and worse, deceiving and being deceived. But you must continue in the things which you have learned and been assured of, knowing from whom you have learned them, and that from childhood you have known the Holy Scriptures, which are able to make you wise for salvation through faith which is in Christ Jesus. All Scripture is given by inspiration of God, and is profitable for doctrine, for reproof, for correction, for instruction in righteousness, that the man of God may be complete, thoroughly equipped for every good work" 2 Timothy 3:10-17. As a child Timothy received instruction in the scriptures from his mother Eunice who had been schooled by her mother Lois. This family heritage became the platform upon which the Apostle Paul gave Timothy training in ministry.

*D*iscipline

The second premise for honor is discipline. Discipline is how the values of heritage are enforced. One day as a teenager I was playing with a soccer ball at home by myself and a hard kick sent the ball over the fence and broke the louver glass window of our neighbor. I was frightened and run into the house hoping that no one would know I was responsible. Later that evening the door bell rang and it was our neighbor asking for the owner of the soccer ball and my slippers that I had left behind when I fled from the incident. She told my parents that assuming I had come to own up for the damage to her window, she would have forgiven me and not reported the incident. When she left my dad chastened me with a cane on my palm. The reason for the punishment was that I should never turn my back on a problem I have caused. Though a leader may be diligent to establish rules and values in their constituency or organization, without enforcement people would trample upon them. "And you have forgotten the exhortation which speaks to you as to sons: "My son, do not despise the chastening of the Lord, Nor be discouraged when you are rebuked by Him; For whom the Lord loves He chastens, And scourges every son whom He receives." If you endure chastening, God deals with you as with sons; for what son is there whom a father does not chasten? But if you are without chastening, of which all have become partakers, then you are illegitimate and not sons. Furthermore, we have had human fathers who corrected us, and we paid them respect. Shall we not much more readily be in subjection to the Father of spirits and live? For they indeed for a few days chastened us as seemed best to them, but He for our profit, that we may be partakers of His holiness. Now no chastening seems to be joyful for the present, but painful; nevertheless, afterward it yields the peaceable fruit of righteousness to those who have been trained by it. Therefore strengthen the hands which hang down, and the feeble knees, and make straight paths for your feet, so that what is lame may not be dislocated, but rather be healed" Hebrews 12:5-12.

First of all the word 'chastening' used in this scripture is the essence of discipline. The process of discipline may include public correction, verbal rebuke, denial of benefits and scourging. For some people verbal instruction and warnings do not serve as a deterrent for breaking rules. They act as though their ears only serve for decoration! For such people, the only way by which instructions make sense is when some form of discipline is applied to their defaulting. Secondly, the scripture above said in verse 6 - "For whom the Lord loves He chastens, And scourges every son whom He receives." The love of God necessitates our chastening. A parent that does not apply chastening as a means to maintain order fails to demonstrate love. Many parents in society today fail to discipline their children because they assume that it is not an act of love. As a result, many children grow and mature in waywardness and extremism. There is a thin line between discipline and abuse. While discipline is a tool of correction, abuse takes place when a person in position of authority exerts pain or embarrassment to others excessively for their own pleasure. Where some pain is administered for discipline it must be limited in scope. Thirdly, chastening has the potential of correcting some bloodline issues. "Therefore strengthen the hands which hang down, and the feeble knees, and make straight paths for your feet, so that what is lame may not be dislocated, but rather be healed." (Hebrews 12:12,13) The pain or embarrassment of chastening sends a signal of restraint to the mind. A stimulus of caution is triggered whenever there is an allure to violate the values of one's heritage. This way the eggs of lust in the emotion get suppressed and may not be conceived by the tempter. Discipline under normal circumstances, introduces an instinct to resist the temptation to do wrong.

ℬosterity

The third premise of honor is posterity. Posterity is a reference to descendants. Our unique individual abilities are ancestrally inherited. God endowed Adam the first man with all the potential abilities of mankind. Adam's descendants receive a piece of these potentials as God assigns each man an anointing. "But you have an anointing from the Holy One, and you know all things... But the anointing which you have received from Him abides in you, and you do not need that anyone teach you; but as the same anointing teaches you concerning all things, and is true, and is not a lie, and just as it has taught you, you will abide in Him" 1 John 2:20&27. The anointing makes us creative in our divine calling. Parents groom their children and mentors prepare their protégé to develop a relationship with the anointing. Fatherhood equips us to develop our seven senses - intuition, discernment, vision, prophecy, audition, comprehension and conviction. A classic example is the story of Samuel serving under Eli the high priest of Israel. "Now the boy Samuel ministered to the Lord before Eli. And the word of the Lord was rare in those days; there was no widespread revelation. And it came to pass at that time, while Eli was lying down in his place, and when his eyes had begun to grow so dim that he could not see, and before the lamp of God went out in the tabernacle of the Lord where the ark of God was, and while Samuel was lying down, that the Lord called Samuel. And he answered, "Here I am!" So he ran to Eli and said, "Here I am, for you called me." And he said, "I did not call; lie down again." And he went and lay down. Then the Lord called yet again, "Samuel!" So Samuel arose and went to Eli, and said, "Here I am, for you called me." He answered, "I did not call, my son; lie down again." (Now Samuel did not yet know the Lord, nor was the word of the Lord yet revealed to him.) And the Lord called Samuel again the third time. So he arose and went to Eli, and said, "Here I am, for you did call me." Then Eli perceived that the Lord had called the boy. Therefore Eli said to

Samuel, "Go, lie down; and it shall be, if He calls you, that you must say, Speak, Lord, for Your servant hears.'" So Samuel went and lay down in his place. Now the Lord came and stood and called as at other times, "Samuel! Samuel!" And Samuel answered, "Speak, for Your servant hears" 1 Samuel 3:1-10.

When God spoke to Samuel for the first time, he was not acquainted to hearing from God so he mistook God for Eli. After repeated instances of the occurrence, Eli perceives that God wanted to communicate directly to Samuel so he coaches Samuel on how to respond to God. Godly leaders have the responsibility of coaching their protégé to develop a relationship with the anointing and then cut them loose to flourish in creativity with God. Unfortunately, some protégé become insolent when they realize they have direct access to God through the anointing. They see no need to honor their kingmakers and start to behave as bastards. "Whoever curses his father or his mother, His lamp will be put out in deep darkness" Proverbs 20:20. To insult, accuse, condemn or disrespect our leaders is how we curse them. Parents as well as leaders often pay a deep price to incubate and nurture their young. Anyone who disrespects their leader suffers the consequence of losing the genuine anointing. When King Saul dishonored Prophet Samuel who was his kingmaker, he lost the true anointing that connected him with God. He became tormented by an evil spirit. Usually the vacuum created by loss of the true anointing of God would be quickly recognized by evil spirits who come to occupy that space and foster perversion.

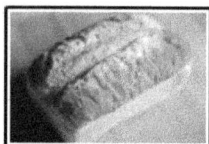

Legacy

The fourth premise of honor is legacy. Technically legacy is the estate passed on to the next generation. It may usually comprise of money or property. "A good man leaves an inheritance to his children's children, but the wealth of the sinner is stored up for the righteous" Proverbs 13:22. "Houses and riches are an inheritance from fathers..." Proverbs 19:14a.

Building a physical estate for one's progeny provides an important jumpstart in life. The scripture records that Abraham the patriarch gave legacy to his progeny. "And Abraham gave all that he had to Isaac. But Abraham gave gifts to the sons of the concubines which Abraham had; and while he was still living he sent them eastward, away from Isaac his son, to the country of the east" Genesis 25:5&6. Abraham bequeathed the larger part of his estate to Isaac and distributed his riches among his children.

Without a legacy people have to engage in meager employment service or start a small enterprise to build an estate. It is no easy road at all! To own property, you will have to start off as a peasant, paying rents and royalties until you can save enough money to purchase property. Jesus told the parable of the prodigal son from which we learn the essence of building wealth.

"Then He said: "A certain man had two sons. And the younger of them said to his father, 'Father, give me the portion of goods that falls to me.' So he divided to them his livelihood. And not many days after, the younger son gathered all together, journeyed to a far country, and there wasted his possessions with prodigal living. But when he had spent all, there arose a severe famine in that land, and he began to be in want. Then he went and joined himself to a citizen of that country, and he sent him into his fields to feed swine. And he would gladly have filled his stomach with the pods that the swine ate, and no one gave him anything. "But when he came to himself, he said, 'How many of my father's hired servants have bread enough and to spare, and I perish with hunger! I will arise and go to my father, and will say to him, "Father, I have sinned against heaven and before you, and I am no longer worthy to be called your son. Make me like one of your hired servants."' "And he arose and came to his father. But when he was still a great way off, his father saw him and had compassion, and ran and fell

on his neck and kissed him. And the son said to him,
'Father, I have sinned against heaven and in your
sight, and am no longer worthy to be called your son.'
"But the father said to his servants, 'Bring out the best
robe and put it on him, and put a ring on his hand
and sandals on his feet. And bring the fatted calf here
and kill it, and let us eat and be merry; for this my son
was dead and is alive again; he was lost and is found.'
And they began to be merry" Luke 15:11-24.

The lack of a culture of savings and investment are
two core reasons for the downfall of the prodigal son.
First of all, he liquidated his assets from the family
estate prematurely, and secondly he squandered the
money. Though they may sound the same to many, it
is important to understand the difference between
savings and investment. Savings is a buildup of money
in a bank account that may earn some form of annual
interest. On the other hand, investment is to seed into
a business venture so as to participate in the profits.
While savings accounts usually promise a fixed rate of
interest as annual returns, there is no limit to what
may be earned from an investment. Furthermore, a
real wealth investment is to seed in a venture that is
connected to one's calling or anointing. Those who
often seed into ventures that reflect their calling
position themselves to enjoy the blessing of
restoration that comes during the jubilee to end
disinheritance. Though savings is the first step when
we start building our financial resources, at a certain

threshold it must be converted into an investment that reflects one's anointing. Many financial institutions have the habit of masking savings products to look like investments. It is also important to note many financial products offered as savings and investments are deliberately designed in a complex way to confuse potential clients. This way, most clients end up assigning the entire portfolio of their finances to brokers who may often end up benefiting more. Rockefeller, Carnegie and J. P. Morgan are names synonymous with wealth legacies here in America. Though they have all passed on, the abundance they accrued through their work is passed on to their progeny. The stories of these wealthy families demonstrate that a culture of savings and investment is cardinal to wealth building.

6

The Culture of Life

"You shall not murder"
Exodus 20:13

The Oklahoma City bombings, Columbine High School massacre, Virginia Tech shootings and Sandy Hook Elementary School Shootings among others are all tragic memories of the devaluation of human life in society today. It is no news that there is a crisis of unjustifiable murder here in the United States. According to FBI Statistics, in 2015 the number of officially recorded murders in the United States was 15,696. The report also indicates that this was a significant increase from the previous year. The causes for traditional murder are usually related to robbery, gang-activity and aggravated assault. Compounding the murder crisis is the syndrome of wrongful convictions that has led to an alarming rate of unjust

111

incarcerations. The causes for wrongful convictions have been identified as including eyewitness misidentification, junk science, false confessions, government misconduct, snitches and incompetent legal advocates. For all of its consequences to victims, wrongful conviction is a form of systemic murder that plagues our society. We also find this evident in the business world where profiteering through the production and sales of potentially life-impairing food, drugs and such inventions also constitute a form of murder.

The first recorded murder in the scriptures was committed by the firstborn son of Adam and Eve. "Now Adam knew Eve his wife, and she conceived and bore Cain, and said, "I have acquired a man from the Lord." Then she bore again, this time his brother Abel. Now Abel was a keeper of sheep, but Cain was a tiller of the ground. And in the process of time it came to pass that Cain brought an offering of the fruit of the ground to the Lord. Abel also brought of the firstborn of his flock and of their fat. And the Lord respected Abel and his offering, but He did not respect Cain and his offering. And Cain was very angry, and his countenance fell. So the Lord said to Cain, "Why are you angry? And why has your countenance fallen? If you do well, will you not be accepted? And if you do not do well, sin lies at the door. And its desire is for you, but you should rule over it." Now Cain talked with Abel his brother; and it came to pass, when they were in the field, that Cain rose up against Abel his brother and killed him. Then the Lord said to Cain, "Where is Abel your brother?" He said, "I do not know. Am I my brother's keeper?" And He said, "What have you done? The voice of your brother's blood cries out to Me from the ground. So now you are cursed from the earth, which has opened its mouth to receive your brother's blood from your hand. When you till the ground, it shall no longer yield its strength to you. A fugitive and a vagabond you shall be on the earth" Genesis 4:1-12.

Cain and Abel who were offspring of Adam and Eve decided to offer a sacrifice to God. Abel's sacrifice was accepted because it met certain standards – firstling, flock and fat. All through the scriptures we find these as the requirements of an acceptable offering to God. Cain obviously did not apply these standards to his sacrifice and so it was not accepted. Cain's attitude is very common among many Christians today who want to honor God on their own terms. When Cain's sacrifice was not accepted, he got angry and went about with a downcast attitude! God noticed Cain's demeanor and approached him with a solution – "If you do well, will you not be accepted?" Simply put, just do the right thing! Comply with the standard and your sacrifice would be accepted. Furthermore, God advised Cain about the consequence of a fallen countenance – "And if you do not do well, sin lies at the door. And its desire is for you, but you should rule over it." Continual brooding over what wrongs have happened in the past may open the door to Satan's inspired nature (sin). Cain did not heed the admonishment of God and murdered Abel. The consequence of his actions invoked upon him the curse of a fugitive and vagabond.

The essence of the sixth commandment is the preservation of human life. The life of every human being is very precious, and we must all strive for the sustenance of one another. Compliance, forgiveness, purpose and destiny are four opportunities to express life and overcome the allure of murder.

Compliance

While living up to certain set standards or rules may come easy for some people, to others it comes as a challenge. Most often those who were not raised up in a framework of order, find it hard to conform to some of the standards that may be required of them. There is a tendency that they become discontented and resentful of those who through compliance have achieved some good things. A rigged standard may also trigger discontentment in those who feel cheated by the system. Prejudice is the root of several injustices including murder that was meted out in the past to individuals of minority group origin in the North American population. Sadly, some police officers as well as white supremacist groups are notorious for many unwarranted arbitrary execution-style murders. Systemic deprivation of the African American community in the aftermaths of the slavery era is root cause of some of the gang activity that is prevalent in the inner-cites. Unemployed young men who may lack opportunity, cash in on the drug wave for survival but then end up in gang-related activities.

Sheer greed, prejudice as well as discontentment often cause people to become rogues. A rogue is someone who violates the established standards arbitrarily and murder is the ultimate act. There are two sides to the coin when it comes to rogues. From political leaders to industry leaders, the promulgation of queer rules that foster a bias against some targeted groups in society is rogue activity that breeds rogues on the other side of the coin. Unhinged rules and standards in any society push the discontented against the wall for which reason they try to find a way for survival. For instance, during the era of prohibition, the Mafia thrived exceedingly in the business of bootlegged liquor. At the time, street executions and cold-blooded murder were rampart. It is worthwhile to note that after the laws of prohibition were ended, this core revenue base of the mafia was obliterated.

Every environment has rules by which those who reside may flourish. Without rules and standards there would be chaos that makes any community feel like an atmosphere of hell. When Adam and Eve violated the instruction concerning the 'tree of the knowledge of good and evil' they were expelled from the Garden of Eden. Their intimate relationship with God came to an end and they had to survive in a hostile environment outside the garden. God was compassionate upon their offspring Cain and Abel and desired to ameliorate their condition by giving them another opportunity to experience the life of God. The solution was to present an acceptable sacrifice. The life of God is how we unleash the great divine potentials that reside within us as human beings.

"For this commandment which I command you today is not too mysterious for you, nor is it far off. It is not in heaven, that you should say, 'Who will ascend into heaven for us and bring it to us, that we may hear it and do it?' Nor is it beyond the sea, that you should say, 'Who will go over the sea for us and bring it to us, that we may hear it and do it?' But the word is very near you, in your mouth and in your heart, that you may do it. "See, I have set before you today life and good, death and evil, in that I command you today to love the Lord your God, to walk in His ways, and to keep His commandments, His statutes, and His judgments, that you may live and multiply; and the Lord your God will bless you in the land which you go to possess. But if your heart turns away so that you do not hear, and are drawn away, and worship other gods and serve them, I announce to you today that you shall surely perish; you shall not prolong your days in the land which you cross over the Jordan to go in and possess. I call heaven and earth as witnesses today against you, that I have set before you life and death, blessing and cursing; therefore choose life, that both you and your descendants   may   live; that   you   may   love the Lord your God, that you may obey His voice, and that you may cling to Him, for He is your life and the length of your days; and that you may dwell in the land   which   the Lord swore   to   your   fathers,   to Abraham,   Isaac,   and   Jacob,   to   give   them" Deuteronomy 30:11-20.

God's   standards   are   neither   mysterious   nor burdensome. They are simple codes of conduct that elevate us beyond an animalistic existence. Divine standards of godliness feed our conscience with the ability to identify and demonstrate the life of God. For instance, when a developer builds a residential estate or office, or retail facility, rules and regulations are established for tenants. The reason for these rules is never to punish the tenants but that everyone would conduct themselves with decency and orderliness. This way we can preserve the property and its utilities for everyone to enjoy. In the same way, divine standards are never meant to punish or inhibit people. Rather they enable us to conform to the life of God that unleashes our potentials for excellence.

Forgiveness

The emotion of anger is a natural reaction when someone violates the standards or rules of an environment. At some point, even the greatest Saint gets angry because someone's rogue action has orchestrated an unnecessary problem. The Apostle Paul is clear about this in the scriptures – "Be angry, and do not sin": do not let the sun go down on your wrath" Ephesians 4:26. Anger must be controlled and limited to a moment. When the emotion of anger is allowed to continue unabated, it degenerates into bitterness, malice or hate and ultimately results in an act of vengeance. The virtue of forgiveness is the breaking point that places a limitation on anger, bitterness, malice or hatred. Forgiveness is the act of pardoning somebody for a mistake or wrongdoing. The greatest act of forgiveness was by our Lord Jesus

Christ who while on the cross of crucifixion prayed – "Father, forgive them, for they do not know what they do" Luke 23:34. He interceded for those who executed him. Jesus pleaded for their leniency with the Father who judges everyone according to their deeds. He contested that their actions were based on ignorance. This was a true demonstration of what he taught his disciples concerning forgiveness. "For if you forgive men their trespasses, your heavenly Father will also forgive you. But if you do not forgive men their trespasses, neither will your Father forgive your trespasses" Matthew 6:14&15. The rule here is that forgiveness of men invokes forgiveness with God. People who hurt us, do not have to beg for forgiveness before we pardon them. Forgiveness is like a seed we ought always to be prepared to sow because it increases God's graciousness upon our lives.

Cain passed on a heritage of murder to his descendants and so wickedness became prevalent in society. "Then Lamech said to his wives: "Adah and Zillah, hear my voice; Wives of Lamech, listen to my speech! For I have killed a man for wounding me, Even a young man for hurting me. If Cain shall be avenged sevenfold, Then Lamech seventy-sevenfold" Genesis 4:23&24. Lamech was a descendant of Cain and he testifies to killing someone who hurt him. Like his ancestor Cain he was unable forgive and control his anger, so the consequence was murder. With approximately half of society carrying the instincts of Cain, society became badly corrupted with so much crime. God intervened and judged humanity by a flood in the days of Noah. The members of Noah's family were the only survivors. When the flood was over, God established an ordinance with man.

"Every moving thing that lives shall be food for you. I have given you all things, even as the green herbs. But you shall not eat flesh with its life, that is, its blood. Surely for your lifeblood I will demand a reckoning; from the hand of every beast I will require it, and from the hand of man. From the hand of every man's brother I will require the life of man. "Whoever sheds man's blood, By man his blood shall be shed; For in the image of God He made man"
Genesis 9:4-6.

This ordinance of God unveils important truths about blood, animal life and human life. Blood is the essence of life here on earth. Animal blood must not be eaten as food. Human blood must not be shed intentionally. The distinction between an animal and man is that though our existence on earth is sustained by blood, we humans were made in the image of God. While animals function primarily on instincts that travel their bloodline, man is a more complex being with a sophisticated conscience, emotions, intellect and will. Animals are limited to instinctive actions within the faculty of the emotion. Humans are made in the image of God not just to react to our instincts but to also make intelligent decisions and exercise our will. This is the reason that we humans are progressive and develop a civil society while animals remain unchanged in their habitats. Though the fall of Adam relegates us to biological life, salvation in Christ Jesus gives us the opportunity of redemption which enhances us with the life of God. "For as in Adam all die, even so in Christ all shall be made alive" 1 Corinthians 15:22. "For the wages of sin is death, but the gift of God is eternal life in Christ Jesus our Lord" Romans 6:23.

The word for animal and human life is 'bios' as distinct from the new life given by Christ to those who are saved that comes from the Greek word 'zoe'. Zoe is a Christ-centered life that entails being transformed into the image of God. For instance, as Christ forgave we also forgive those who trespass against us. "And this is the testimony: that God has given us eternal life, and this life is in His Son. He who has the Son has life; he who does not have the Son of God does not have life. These things I have written to you who believe in the name of the Son of God, that you may know that you have eternal life, and that you may continue to believe in the name of the Son of God" 1 John 5:11-13. The life that God intends for everyone is what Jesus Christ modeled for us while on earth. If only we would embrace it, the grace to live the life of God was unleashed upon humanity at the cross of Christ's crucifixion. Remember when Stephen was being stoned for his testimony of Christ, he exemplified this grace. "Then they cried out with a loud voice, stopped their ears, and ran at him with one accord; and they cast him out of the city and stoned him. And the witnesses laid down their clothes at the feet of a young man named Saul. And they stoned Stephen as he was calling on God and saying, "Lord Jesus, receive my spirit." Then he knelt down and cried out with a loud voice, "Lord, do not charge them with this sin." And when he had said this, he fell asleep" Acts 7:57-60. Stephen demonstrated an unusual grace of forgiveness that has been bestowed upon all believers who would embrace it. The dispensation of grace which is this era in which we live in, mandates us to demonstrate graciousness towards one another.

As far back as during the Old Testament era, God made provision for atonement so that man would not remain cut off from his life. "And whatever man of the house of Israel, or of the strangers who dwell among you, who eats any blood, I will set My face against that person who eats blood, and will cut him off from among his people. For the life of the flesh is in the blood, and I have given it to you upon the altar to make atonement for your souls; for it is the blood that makes atonement for the soul.' Therefore I said to the children of Israel, 'No one among you shall eat blood, nor shall any stranger who dwells among you eat blood" Leviticus 17:10-12. Animal blood was accepted for atonement of the soul of man because God wanted man to have a way of relating to him even when we have become victims of sin. God yearns to maintain fellowship with us. "But Christ came as High Priest of the good things to come, with the greater and more perfect tabernacle not made with hands, that is, not of this creation. Not with the blood of goats and calves, but with His own blood He entered the Most Holy Place once for all, having obtained eternal redemption. For if the blood of bulls and goats and the ashes of a heifer, sprinkling the unclean, sanctifies for the purifying of the flesh, how much more shall the blood of Christ, who through the eternal Spirit offered Himself without spot to God, cleanse your conscience from dead works to serve the living God? And for this reason He is the Mediator of the new covenant, by means of death, for the redemption of the transgressions under the first covenant, that those who are called may receive the promise of the eternal inheritance" Hebrews 9:11-15. The blood of Jesus is the perfect sacrifice that breaks down the wall of hostility between us and God. All the self-imposed curses, the evil we executed against others including cursing, wickedness and murder have been atoned for by the blood of Jesus that flowed on the cross of Calvary. We can forgive others and also receive forgiveness and the blessing of eternal life in Christ Jesus.

Purpose

When a person's anger degenerates into bitterness or malice the next stage is rage or fury. Fury is expressed in violent acts that may include destruction and murder. Most often when people display fury, it is as though they are possessed. They act animalistic. In the same way we are anointed to fulfill our divine purpose, fury is usually demonic inspired. Those under demonic influence only feel sober after the act of fury is discharged and they are faced with the consequence of what just happened.

The reason for which we were all created is divine purpose. Each individual person has a unique role to play in life that compliments all others. While we may attempt to assign any mission that may seem convenient to ourselves, it is only God that can reveal the purpose of man. Purpose is God's original intent for any man. It is the conduit through which God streams creativity into our being.

Purpose is the bedrock of human creativity. As we learnt in the previous chapter, mentors groom their protégé to function in the anointing of their purpose.

A core privilege of a leader or mentor is to impart blessings upon their protégé when sending them off. Out of fury, some mentors have pronounced curses that had a damaging effect upon their protégé. Several years ago a young man by name Robert was a mechanic who used to fix my car. He was very good at altering difficult problems but there was a problem that consistently marred his work. When the repair work on the car was completed, he would either leave a tool in the engine or forget to tighten a bolt or do something entirely awkward. When I noticed this pattern of occurrences, I called him to have a talk. I asked him if he properly graduated from apprenticeship and the answer was 'no'. It became obvious that his master may have cursed him so I advised him to go back to his master and make peace.

A curse can alter the blessed function of the anointing if the victim is really guilty. Curses are like launching a murder weapon because they potentially terminate the positive impact that God intends for those who are anointed. Blessings on the contrary have the power to unleash the anointing resident in a person so they can fulfill the life God intended. The Apostle Paul impacted his protégé Timothy this way: "Therefore I remind you to stir up the gift of God which is in you through the laying on of my hands. For God has not given us a spirit of fear, but of power and of love and of a sound mind. Therefore do not be ashamed of the testimony of our Lord, nor of me His prisoner, but share with me in the sufferings for the gospel according to the power of God, who has saved us and called us with a holy calling, not according to our works, but according to His own purpose and grace which was given to us in Christ Jesus before time began, but has now been revealed by the appearing of our Savior Jesus Christ, who has abolished death and brought life and immortality to light through the gospel, to which I was appointed a preacher, an apostle, and a teacher of the Gentiles. For this reason I also suffer these things; nevertheless I am not ashamed, for I know whom I have believed and am persuaded that He is able to keep what I have committed to Him until that Day" 2 Timothy 1:6-12.

One core mission of Jesus Christ was the abolishment of death by His victory at the cross of Calvary. We have also received divine life and immortality so that we can fulfill divine purpose to the glory of God.

Destiny

Cain became a fugitive and a vagabond because of his actions contrary to divine purpose. A fugitive is one constantly fleeing from justice while a vagabond is a restless wanderer. This was not the destiny God designed for him but then Abel's blood cried for justice. "And He said, "What have you done? The voice of your brother's blood cries out to Me from the ground. So now you are cursed from the earth, which has opened its mouth to receive your brother's blood from your hand. When you till the ground, it shall no longer yield its strength to you. A fugitive and a vagabond you shall be on the earth." And Cain said to the Lord, "My punishment is greater than I can bear! Surely You have driven me out this day from the face of the ground; I shall be hidden from Your face; I shall be a fugitive and a vagabond on the earth, and it will happen that anyone who finds me will kill me." And the Lord said to him, "Therefore, whoever kills Cain, vengeance shall be taken on him sevenfold." And the Lord set a mark on Cain, lest anyone finding him should kill him" Genesis 4:10-15.

Interestingly when Cain cried to God to invoke mercy, God was entreated. Though there were few humans living on earth, Cain knew that the spirits present could execute the punishment for his act of murder. Prior to the flood of Noah's day, the spirits in those days manifested physically and had interaction with people. If God placed a mark on Cain to preserve him from summary execution, how much more would God extend his compassion and ameliorate our guilt if only we reach out to him sincerely.

The ultimate end of purpose is destiny. Life is a journey that is earmarked with destinations. Assuming we pursue our divine purpose then the destinations are always good and fulfilling. "And we know that all things work together for good to those who love God, to those who are the called according to His purpose. For whom He foreknew, He also predestined to be conformed to the image of His Son, that He might be the firstborn among many brethren. Moreover whom He predestined, these He also called; whom He called, these He also justified; and whom He justified, these He also glorified" Romans 8:28-30. When we walk in our calling, He justifies us and ultimately glorifies us. God predestines us to conform to the image of Christ by righteousness, forgiveness and functioning in the anointing.

1

The Culture of Morality

"You shall not commit adultery"
Exodus 20:14

America is saddled with deep issues of family dysfunction, a very high divorce rate and marriage redefinition. More than half of all marriages whether Christian or non-Christian ends up in divorce. A popular preacher recently characterized marriage as going to a dealership to procure a Cadillac and assuming you do not like it, you trade it in for another! Today so many children are born out of wedlock and single parents are unable to throw in the balance required for the upbringing of their offspring. While not too long ago, sodomy was considered an illegal act punishable by imprisonment, recently the federal government has legalized same sex marriage. We are currently groping with the issues of

131

heterosexuals in society and I suspect bestiality may be next.

Marriage is the relationship between a man and woman. It was the first institution God established in the beginning. "And the Lord God said, "It is not good that man should be alone; I will make him a helper comparable to him." … So Adam gave names to all cattle, to the birds of the air, and to every beast of the field. But for Adam there was not found a helper comparable to him. And the Lord God caused a deep sleep to fall on Adam, and he slept; and He took one of his ribs, and closed up the flesh in its place. Then the rib which the Lord God had taken from man He made into a woman, and He brought her to the man. And Adam said: "This is now bone of my bones And flesh of my flesh; She shall be called Woman, Because she was taken out of Man." Therefore a man shall leave his father and mother and be joined to his wife, and they shall become one flesh. And they were both naked, the man and his wife, and were not ashamed" Genesis 2:18,20-25. This scripture articulates clearly the origin, nature and purpose of marriage. Marriage is God's solution for intra-human relationship, counsel and procreation. To redefine marriage any other way than originally intended by God is to foster immorality and grave consequences to society. Most of the difficult challenges in society today can be traced to the breakdown of the family structure.

The seventh commandment is the essence of a moral standard in society. Without a standard there is no pillar upon which we hinge our morality. Adultery is to have intercourse outside of wedlock. It embodies the perpetuation of sexual lust, perversions and ultimately family dysfunctions.

Marriage

The union between a man and woman is the core moral standard of human society and every other institution can only thrive upon this foundation. As a pastor, one of my core responsibilities is to groom potential couples ahead of the solemnization of the holy matrimony. The grooming process involves helping the couple to develop their intrapersonal relationship. The man is made aware of how to interact with typical female emotions while the lady learns how to deal with the male personality. Lessons learned in this grooming process transcends the marriage and helps married people manage relationships with the opposite sex better in other contexts such as the work place and community. Post marriage counseling services are also available to help couples deal with complex situations that arise during marriage. Typically, judges will not sign off on a divorce unless there is a period of separation during which the couple may rethink their resolution and probably seek counseling. While there is no perfect man or woman, marriage is a learning process for every human. "Wives, likewise, be submissive to your own husbands, that even if some do not obey the word, they, without a word, may be won by the conduct of their wives, when they observe your chaste conduct accompanied by fear. Do not let your adornment be merely outward—arranging the hair, wearing gold, or putting on fine apparel— rather let it be the hidden person of the heart, with the incorruptible beauty of a meek and quiet spirit, which is very precious in the sight of God. For in this manner, in former times, the holy women who trusted in God also adorned themselves, being submissive to their own husbands, as Sarah obeyed Abraham, calling him lord, whose daughters you are if you do good and are not afraid with any terror. Husbands, likewise, dwell with them with understanding, giving honor to the wife, as to the weaker vessel, and as being heirs together of the grace of life, that your prayers may not be hindered" 1 Peter 3:1-7. 'Power struggle' is the root of many of the problems that confront and ultimately end business partnerships, political unions, social groups, church affiliations and so on. A godly marriage is the framework for developing the power of influence resident in us. Regardless of where you stand in the pivot of leadership, we all have the potential to wield power.

The Apostle Paul admonishes wives who are deputy of their husbands in the framework of marriage to demonstrate submission and model God's word as a lifestyle. Several years ago, as a young and unmarried pastor, I had to help people who were victims of spousal abuse. With no actual experience in marriage life I had to rely on the scriptures and to my amazement it always provided great results. The spouse who felt victimized was usually the one who sought help. A spouse who victimizes the other is usually reacting to unacceptable actions. The solution is for the victimized to foster change by demonstrating the lifestyle of righteousness prescribed by the scriptures. Assuming a husband is abusing his wife by flirting with other ladies, it would not be a smart approach to engage in a beauty pageant to upgrade one's appeal. Neither should a wife attempt to tone her muscles and procure boxing gloves to match her husband 'pound for pound'. While experiencing abuse from their husbands, some wives seek counsel from friends who may typically advice them to display strength and fight back. This tactic hardly works with men. The key is to develop the virtues of a meek and quiet spirit. Meekness and a quite spirit are attributes that manifest the femininity of a woman. To be meek means submissiveness while a quite spirit is the disposition of being gentle. These qualities are core to inner beauty which appreciates with time. This means that though a woman may lose her physical attraction as she grows older, the inner beauty should appreciate to make it up. If women focus on developing their inner beauty, their appeal grows with their husbands. Unfortunately, with many married women, the 'tragedy of familiarity' costs them their inner allure which in turn alienates their husbands. I have observed over the years that if one spouse would endeavor to do the right thing in the eyes of God, it is possible the marriage can be fixed supernaturally. "For the unbelieving husband is sanctified by the wife, and the unbelieving wife is sanctified by the husband; otherwise your children would be unclean, but now they are holy. But if the unbeliever departs, let him depart; a brother or a sister is not under bondage in such cases. But God has called us to peace. For how do you know, O wife, whether you will save your husband? Or how do you know, O husband, whether you will save your wife?" 1 Corinthians 7:14-16. Marriage is a supernatural union where the 'two become one flesh'. They would only drown if both spouses violate the fundamentals of the marriage union. Most often it is difficult to convince the victim of spousal abuse that they may be responsible for triggering the abuse although this may not be true with all cases. However, the key to divine intervention is for the victim to first fix themselves in the eyes of God. This includes conformity with the standards of the scriptures for a godly marriage union. Assuming the abusive spouse is not repentant, they would simply move on with divorce which would free the abused spouse to move on with their life. However, if the abuse was a reaction of the husband to actions of the wife, the display of the virtues of meekness and a quiet spirit invokes God's intervention so the marriage is restored.

When it comes to husbands, the scripture says – "Husbands, likewise, dwell with them with understanding, giving honor to the wife, as to the weaker vessel, and as being heirs together of the grace of life, that your prayers may not be hindered" 1 Peter 3:7. To be a good husband, a man must embrace the essence of understanding, honor and partnership in marriage. Understanding is to have insight of knowledge. Simply put, a husband must be knowledgeable and constantly upgrade himself by learning from books or attending seminars. He must not be ignorant. Beware of a man who does not read and only learns from the street! Street knowledge is not good enough for the CEO of your family. You do not want to be a victim of street justice in your home! Secondly, a husband must honor his wife. As we learnt earlier on, honor is to have dignity and respect. Without dignity which is self-worth it is almost impossible to respect the value in others. A good husband must have a heritage, be noble, have regard for posterity and build a legacy for the family. Finally, a potentially good husband sees his wife as a life-partner. He has not married a slave to his ambition but aspires to build a synergy for their corporate good. She is a helpmate in pursuit of a common destiny and so stands side-by-side and not under his feet.

Love

The English language appropriates the word 'love' for several contexts of affection which though a nuance is distinct in the Greek. The Greek language distinguishes the relationship between friends as 'Phileo', God's love for mankind as 'Agape' and the love between husband and wife as 'Eros'. Our focus here is on 'Eros' love. This kind of love is exclusive between married couples. It is the only framework for sexual relations between a man and woman. Sex outside of marriage is the product of lust. When a married spouse has sex outside their marriage it is considered as adultery. If those having sex are not married, then it is considered as fornication. Today many people do not know the difference between lust and love because lust is commonly called love. As a result, many people are desensitized and cannot tell when they are violating the moral standard. Sexual lust is an appetite for erotic romance and in most cases can be controlled through discipline. It is unfortunate that instead of dealing with issues such as sexually transmitted diseases and unwanted pregnancies which are typical consequences of sexual lust, free condoms are distributed to high school kids. What happened to promoting the value of abstinence and disciplining young people who flout it?

Assuming two people who get married by the proclamation of marriage vows at the court house fail to have sex, the marriage is considered 'not consummated' so can be quickly annulled without legal tussle. Sexual intercourse cannot be casual for those outside a marriage relationship because it has spiritual implications. "...Now the body is not for sexual immorality but for the Lord, and the Lord for the body. And God both raised up the Lord and will also raise us up by His power. Do you not know that your bodies are members of Christ? Shall I then take the members of Christ and make them members of a harlot? Certainly not! Or do you not know that he who is joined to a harlot is one body with her? For "the two," He says, "shall become one flesh." But he who is joined to the Lord is one spirit with Him. Flee sexual immorality. Every sin that a man does is outside the body, but he who commits sexual immorality sins against his own body. Or do

139

you not know that your body is the temple of the Holy Spirit who is in you, whom you have from God, and you are not your own? For you were bought at a price; therefore glorify God in your body and in your spirit, which are God's" 1 Corinthians 6:13b-20.

Sexual intercourse establishes a blood covenant between two people. Blood covenant facilitates interaction and transfer of spirits. In the same way that Christ the bridegroom influences His Church which is His bride, it is possible for the kingdom of darkness to spread lustful spirits through sex outside the marriage union.

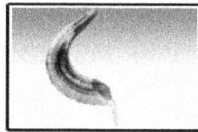

Progeny

Today science facilitates procreation without sexual intercourse. Sperm donors can furnish the female womb through artificial insemination. Children who may never know their biological parents are being bred daily. Who knows where this would end, as ideas of genetically modified humans circulate in science journals and in science-fiction movies. Gay couples have fought for the privilege to adopt and raise children in a perverted environment. For someone raised in a perverse environment, this further compounds the crisis of what constitutes a moral standard in the mind.

Cultural inhibitions, conflicted purposes and emotional frustrations are among the reasons for homosexuality and gender issues. Prior to the development of the ultrasound machine for determining the gender of a baby in the womb of a pregnant woman, expectant mothers often made a wild guess. In certain cultures, the male son was preferred as first-born progeny and so for fear of rejection, expectant mothers would psych themselves for a male child. A woman who also desired a female baby may also psych themselves during pregnancy. Assuming the baby God gives is a different gender than what was expected by a pregnant woman, there is a conflict of purpose. Where the anatomy of the baby in the womb is different from the psychological bearings of the expectant mother, the baby is born with a conflicted gender identity.

A perverse environment defeats the divine purpose for procreation. "And this is the second thing you do: You cover the altar of the Lord with tears, With weeping and crying; So He does not regard the offering anymore, Nor receive it with goodwill from your hands. Yet you say, "For what reason?" Because the Lord has been witness Between you and the wife of your youth, With whom you have dealt treacherously; Yet she is your companion And your wife by covenant. But did He not make them one, Having a remnant of the Spirit? And why one? He seeks godly offspring. Therefore take heed to your spirit, And let none deal treacherously with the wife of his youth. "For the Lord God of Israel says That He hates divorce, For it covers one's garment with violence," Says the Lord of hosts. "Therefore take heed to your spirit, That you do not deal treacherously" Malachi 2:13-16. One of the core purposes of marriage is procreation. God intended the union to produce 'godly offspring'. The story of Laban and Jacob is a classical example of the consequence of procreation from an insincere relationship. As an agreed bride price for Rachael, Jacob served Laban her father for seven years. After the wedding, Jacob realizes that he has been given Leah instead of Rachael. He gets angry and confronts Laban who requests an additional seven years for Rachael. This trickery of Laban does not go down well with Jacob and so he is not able to love Leah though they are formally married. Jacob and Leah conceive three children who are named after the emotional frustrations of Leah. "So Leah conceived and bore a son, and she called his name Reuben; for she said, "The Lord has surely looked on my affliction. Now therefore, my husband will love me." Then she conceived again and bore a son, and said, "Because the Lord has heard that I am unloved,

He has therefore given me this son also." And she called his name Simeon. She conceived again and bore a son, and said, "Now this time my husband will become attached to me, because I have borne him three sons." Therefore his name was called Levi." Genesis 29:32-34. Reuben is named after Leah's affliction and it affects his initial emotional disposition. He causes his father pain and fails to receive the blessings of the firstborn. Simeon the second born is named according to Leah's feelings of hate from Jacob, while the third born Levi's name means 'detachment'. Simeon and Levi brought pain to Jacob through cruel acts that reflect the emotions they inherited while in Leah's womb. A sincere environment of true love and faithfulness is essential for raising progeny.

Family

There is a great divide in America today as to the role of government in the lives of citizens. While some contend that people in crisis should cater for themselves, others say the government should have welfare programs for intervention. It is obvious that both positions have merits in their arguments.

However, it is important for us to ask ourselves what is the root cause of the crisis of those who are homeless in society and wander about looking for food to eat. If we do not take a careful look at laws and institutional structures that contribute to family dysfunction in America, the crisis would only deepen and several years from now, the statistics would only show everyone on both sides as losers in this argument.

The overall moral strength or weakness of any society can be traced directly to the state of the family institution. A family is any group of people who are closely related by birth, marriage, or adoption. For those who belong to a family, it is their natural network of support. Growing up as a young man, I remember several instances where older uncles and aunties were sometimes employed to intervene and counsel a family member who was going astray by their way of life. It always worked and so issues such as truancy, immorality and divorce were corrected locally within the family. If there was death or misfortune of any sort, relatives stepped in to help. Orphans and widows were catered for and not left to survive on their own. Family relatives helped the young graduate get a good job by character referrals and also pooled resources to provide capital for those in pursuit of business ventures. Alibaba.com is among the biggest ecommerce enterprises in the world. The owner Jack Ma tells of how he rallied his relatives to provide the initial seed-capital for the enterprise.

In the scriptures we see how God endorses the family as a framework for basic intra-human support. "And you shall consecrate the fiftieth year, and proclaim liberty throughout all the land to all its inhabitants. It shall be a Jubilee for you; and each of you shall return to his possession, and each of you shall return to his family" Leviticus 25:10. The Jubilee was God's provision for the restoration of family wealth and relationships. It was mandated that all land transactions revolve around the Jubilee so that every family could experience land redemption. In the year of Jubilee all those who were disinherited got a chance at restoration. For many of the custody cases involving children from abusive homes, it is important that the opportunity for foster parenthood be granted foremost to family relatives. This way the burden on the government is reduced and family relationships preserved. There are various ways by which the trends and tendency for government dependency can be addressed without a harsh political stance that may be catastrophic and by its execution very immoral.

8

The Culture of Contentment

"You shall not steal"
Exodus 20:15

Large-scale corporate greed and extortion characterize the landscape of business in America today. Shareholders want more dividends on their investments and so the pressure mounts on corporate executives to find creative ways of exploiting customers. Stringent requirements for basic services that end up as measures to isolate certain classes of the population especially the poor, leave them with no other choice than to be fraudulent in order to qualify for their needs. It is an unfortunate cycle.

"But godliness with contentment is great gain. For we brought nothing into this world, and it is certain we can carry nothing out. And having food and raiment

147

let us be therewith content. But they that will be rich fall into temptation and a snare, and into many foolish and hurtful lusts, which drown men in destruction and perdition. For the love of money is the root of all evil: which while some coveted after, they have erred from the faith, and pierced themselves through with many sorrows" 1 Timothy 6:6-10.

Contentment is the essence of the eighth commandment. It means gratification or calm satisfaction. Our basic necessities of life are food, shelter and clothing. Food sustains our body while shelter and clothing protect us from the environment. The civilization of today makes our lives very complex such that we need several things such as telephones, computers and vehicles for our basic existence. The Apostle Paul is teaching Timothy the essence of being able to define what constitutes our basic needs and focus our efforts on these. We cannot become affectionate with money. "For the love of money is the root of all evil." Our love must be directed primarily towards God who gives us all things to enjoy. Our duty is to engage good stewardship over the blessings that God gives us. Increase and abundance are inevitable where good stewardship is evident.

Jesus used the parable of the unjust steward to illustrate stewardship and I gained some insights on the following text from the teachings of Bishop

Tudor Bismarck. "He also said to His disciples: "There was a certain rich man who had a steward, and an accusation was brought to him that this man was wasting his goods. So he called him and said to him, 'What is this I hear about you? Give an account of your stewardship, for you can no longer be steward.' "Then the steward said within himself, 'What shall I do? For my master is taking the stewardship away from me. I cannot dig; I am ashamed to beg. I have resolved what to do, that when I am put out of the stewardship, they may receive me into their houses.' "So he called every one of his master's debtors to him, and said to the first, 'How much do you owe my master?' And he said, 'A hundred measures of oil.' So he said to him, 'Take your bill, and sit down quickly and write fifty.' Then he said to another, 'And how much do you owe?' So he said, 'A hundred measures of wheat.' And he said to him, 'Take your bill, and write eighty.' So the master commended the unjust steward because he had dealt shrewdly. For the sons of this world are more shrewd in their generation than the sons of light. "And I say to you, make friends for yourselves by unrighteous mammon, that when you fail, they may receive you into an everlasting home. He who is faithful in what is least is faithful also in much; and he who is unjust in what is least is unjust also in much. Therefore if you have not been faithful in the unrighteous mammon, who will commit to your trust the true riches? And if you have not been faithful in what is another man's, who will give you what is your own?" Luke 16:1-12.

This steward was about to lose his job and his thoughts reveal two stages in the progression of stewardship, which are begging and digging. Jesus adds the next two stages of stewardship "Therefore if you have not been faithful in the unrighteous mammon, who will commit to your trust the true riches?" The 'unrighteous mammon' is the stage of riches while 'true riches' means wealth.

Begging is a state of dependency and is sustained by gratitude. Digging is the state of hard work and is sustained by diligence. Riches are the accumulation of savings from skillful work. Wealth is the ultimate estate of those who are prosperous.

Gratitude

We all start out in life begging for our needs. As children we may not work and so do not earn income. We are often dependent upon parents and guardians until we can earn an income through work. Also when we are unemployed and have to depend upon others or welfare programs, it is a form of begging. At this point in life we must be appreciative of all that we are receiving that we did not earn. The unjust steward said, "I am ashamed to beg." For someone who has become self-sustaining over several years of work, depending on others for handouts is an uncomfortable position. It feels as though one is a child all over again and so can be psychologically demeaning. Assuming you are at the receiving end of what you did not work for, it is your responsibility to show appreciation for what you are given. Those who provide your needs feel appreciated when you thank them. Appreciation can be demonstrated by offering some sort of help or taking up a responsibility that is within our ability. We expect our children to take up a chore at home and those on welfare programs must volunteer to participate in community services. Those who fail to demonstrate appreciation for what they receive for their sustenance may eventually lose that privilege and probably end up as thieves.

As commerce and industry began to pick up steam here in North America, so also was the advent of a notorious Italian group known as the Mafia. Core to their existence was extortion and greed. The Mafia was infamous in perpetuating organized crime and was responsible for many murders. It is important that the culture of appreciation be ingrained in people from infancy at home. This way they develop the mindset of exchange even for the things which appear free in life.

Diligence

Diligence means persistent work. In his thoughts the unjust steward said, "I cannot dig." He was now probably in his fifties as a middle-aged Chief Executive who had been enjoying the comforts of riches for a while. Digging is hard work for new entrants into the labor market. Usually such people are either unskilled, students or graduates that lack the experience to occupy managerial positions. You find young people work at fast-food places like McDonalds, retail jobs at Walmart or menial construction jobs. Though the work is hard, the income is usually low and not far from the minimum wage level. At this level, people earn just enough to meet the basic requirements of life. It is difficult to save and we commonly say 'you are living from paycheck to paycheck'. Unfortunately, many people remain at the digging stage all their lives until retirement. You cannot be blamed for the inability to build significant savings but then you have the responsibility to get the training for building a professional career.

"Be diligent to present yourself approved to God, a worker who does not need to be ashamed, rightly dividing the word of truth" 2 Timothy 2:15. Another translation starts out with the phrase 'study to show yourself approved unto God'. Diligence entails the persistent work of discovering the story to your life. It is the unearthing of the history of life that starts from Adam through Jesus Christ that now flows through your veins. "But without faith it is impossible to please Him, for he who comes to God must believe that He is, and that He is a rewarder of those who diligently seek Him" Hebrews 11:6. It is important to apply ourselves to understand the role of God in the scheme of our existence here on earth. God rewards our diligence in developing a solid relationship with him through Jesus Christ. We must know what to believe for as well as what we must work for in life. Grace provides several benefits that we must learn to take through faith. We cannot suffer infirmities for which Christ already received stripes to secure our healing. We must not suffer under the yoke of curses when Christ has already paid the price so we can become blessed. "Now, therefore, you are no longer strangers and foreigners, but fellow citizens with the saints and members of the household of God" Ephesians 2:19. Salvation in Christ makes us a part of the commonwealth of Israel so we must leverage the blessings of grace to take advantage of all the blessings and opportunities available to us.

Many blessings that God unleashes upon us are available within the framework of times and seasons. "Thus says the Lord: "In an acceptable time I have heard You, And in the day of salvation I have helped You; I will preserve You and give You As a covenant to the people, To restore the earth, To cause them to inherit the desolate heritages; That You may say to the prisoners, 'Go forth,' To those who are in darkness, 'Show yourselves.' "They shall feed along the roads, And their pastures shall be on all desolate heights. They shall neither hunger nor thirst, Neither heat nor sun shall strike them; For He who has mercy on them will lead them, Even by the springs of water He will guide them. I will make each of My mountains a road, And My highways shall be elevated. Surely these shall come from afar; Look! Those from the north and the west, and these from the land of Sinim" Isaiah 49:8-12. Insight of what God is doing in each season is essential to guide us in responsiveness. Typically when it is spring, farmers who have been waiting for the season prepare their soil and sow their seeds. Such farmers are responsive to the season and do due diligence and so get themselves a harvest at the appropriate time. In the same way the weather seasons come in a predictable cycle, God visits us with various blessings cyclically. Doors of opportunities open and close when there are changes in spiritual seasons.

The first way to recognize a season is from God's word that is preached by His ministers. God sends us signals of what He intends to accomplish in our lives through the message He gives to us through His messengers. If we pay careful attention to this message, we know what diligence is required of us so we can benefit from the blessings of the season. Secondly, we may know what God is about to do in a season through the opportunities that come our way. Applying the diligence of the message at Church enables good stewardship of the open doors.

Thirdly, we may know what God is about to do in a season by recognizing unusual challenges that come our way. "How can one enter a strong man's house and plunder his goods, unless he first binds the strong man? And then he will plunder his house" Matthew 12:29. Whenever the enemy realizes that he is about to be dispossessed of something that God has designated for us, he launches a preemptive attack. He reasons that if he can demoralize us through fear, our faith wanes and then we abandon diligence in our relationship with God. Consequently, we deny ourselves of the faith by which we receive from God. When we experience an attack of unusual challenges, our response should be to get in warfare mode and bind the enemy. Jesus said, "And I will give you the keys of the kingdom of heaven, and whatever you bind on earth will be bound in heaven, and whatever you loose on earth will be loosed in heaven" Matthew 16:19. We have authority in Christ to bind any spirit that stands in our way to hinder our blessings. It is a fundamental diligence for us as believers.

Skill

Jesus said, "And if you have not been faithful in what is another man's, who will give you what is your own"? The stage of riches is where we function as professionals or in a management position and earn a decent income. The unjust steward was at this stage when it came to light that he had mismanaged his masters' goods and so his job was on the line. It is obvious that the unjust steward had no savings. Though he was at the stage of riches, he was still living from paycheck to paycheck and had not applied the wisdom to build-up financial savings. He quickly devised an interesting scheme to salvage himself assuming he lost his job. "So he called every one of his master's debtors to him, and said to the first, 'How much do you owe my master?' And he said, 'A hundred measures of oil.' So he said to him, 'Take your bill, and sit down quickly and write fifty.' Then he said to another, 'And how much do you owe?' So he said, 'A hundred measures of wheat.' And he said to him, 'Take your bill, and write eighty.' So the master commended the unjust steward because he had dealt shrewdly." Like the corporate executives of today the unjust steward had exploited the customers of the business and so he decided to make a quick fix to earn some future favors. Jesus used this parable to teach core stewardship truths about how to manage our resources. Everyone is blessed with time, life and material resources.

Firstly, the unjust steward was judicious in managing the time of that moment. Time is a function of divine opportunities that come our way. "To everything there is a season, A time for every purpose under heaven: A time to be born, And a time to die; A time to plant, And a time to pluck what is planted; A time to kill, And a time to heal; A time to break down, And a time to build up; A time to weep, And a time to laugh; A time to mourn, And a time to dance; A time to cast away stones, And a time to gather stones; A time to embrace, And a time to refrain from embracing; A time to gain, And a time to lose; A time to keep, And a time to throw away; A time to tear, And a time to sew; A time to keep silence, And a time to speak; A time to love, And a time to hate; A time of war, And a time of peace. What profit has the worker from that in which he labors? I have seen the God-given task with which the sons of men are to be occupied. He has made everything beautiful in its time. Also He has put eternity in their hearts, except that no one can find out the work that God does from beginning to end" Ecclesiastes 3:1-11. There are twenty-eight times, which are fourteen opposites. For every season, time comes in a pair. If you properly handle the negative manifestation of time, it translates into the positive. For instance, if you sow in tears during the time of seed, you will reap fruits during the time of harvest. When the unjust steward was notified that he must give an account of the business, he immediately recognized that time was against him. It was timeout in the stage of riches and he could lose his job. The thought of demotion to begging or digging were not an option for him. He resolved to move up into the dimension of wealth. To achieve this goal, he had to make up for his mismanagement of the time in employed service. The Apostle Paul in his letter to the Ephesians wrote, "See then that you walk circumspectly, not as fools but as wise, redeeming the time, because the days are evil" Ephesians 5:15&16. The unjust steward thought in his mind that since he had lost favor with his employer, he had to seek to enter into the favor of those he had defrauded by overpricing. These were business owners who might potentially do business with him if he demonstrated repentance and a new lifestyle.

Secondly, the life of a human being is the essence of the anointing within. This anointing is significant of the oil debt of 'a hundred measures of oil' owed by a customer. The unjust steward gave this customer a fifty percent discount. This discount was to fulfill the principle of how we impact others with the anointing. Jesus taught that one of the cardinal rules of life is to "love your neighbor as yourself." In other words, you must love your neighbor with the same measure that you love yourself that is fifty percent.

Thirdly, the unjust steward dealt with another customer, "Then he said to another, 'And how much do you owe?' So he said, 'A hundred measures of wheat.' And he said to him, 'Take your bill, and write eighty.'" He gave a twenty percent discount to the wheat customer. Wheat is significant of material resources. To achieve twenty percent, we must give ten percent of our resources as tithes and an equivalent of additional ten percent in various kinds of offerings. This is how we secure divine financial favor. Jesus taught, "Give and it will be given to you: good measure, pressed down, shaken together, and running over will be put into your bosom. For with the same measure that you use, it will be measured back to you" Luke 6:38. This way the unjust steward fixed his debt of divine financial favor so that when he was out of employment, he could enjoy favor as an entrepreneur.

*P*rudence

Jesus called wealth the dimension of 'true riches'. While it may sound as though the discounts given by the unjust steward to the customers were fraudulent, Jesus said that he was commended for his actions. "So the master commended the unjust steward because he had dealt shrewdly. For the sons of this world are more shrewd in their generation than the sons of light. "And I say to you, make friends for yourselves by unrighteous mammon, that when you fail, they may receive you into an everlasting home." Three actions of the unjust steward earned him commendation. First, he started making an impact on his community with his anointed purpose. Secondly, the unjust steward translated the time of demotion into a time of promotion by making strategic decisions. Finally he made deposits for divine financial favor. This way he managed his crisis in such a way that instead of a fall he set the stage to move up to the next stage of wealth. While the realm of riches is a physical dimension, wealth is a spiritual dimension. The unjust steward was commended because he quickly leveraged the opportunities of the dimension of riches to secure a place in the dimension of wealth.

Some financial institutions today are fond of peddling certain financial products as 'wealth builders'. Fundamentally a wealth product must be linked to ones calling or destiny. Whatever investment is made in a financial product whether it is a stock, bond or mutual fund that is not related to ones' anointing should be considered 'riches'. Wealth is the stage where we institutionalize our calling. Here we build an enterprise and set up sustainable structures and systems. We make investments into landed property and assets to solidify the estate of our destiny.

Strategic relationships are important to consolidate wealth. Isaac entered into strategic relationship with the king of the Philistines who were his landlords. "Then Abimelech came to him from Gerar with Ahuzzath, one of his friends, and Phichol the commander of his army. And Isaac said to them, "Why have you come to me, since you hate me and have sent me away from you?" But they said, "We have certainly seen that the Lord is with you. So we said, 'Let there now be an oath between us, between you and us; and let us make a covenant with you, that you will do us no harm, since we have not touched you, and since we have done nothing to you but good and have sent you away in peace. You are now the blessed of the Lord.'" So he made them a feast, and they ate and drank. Then they arose early in the morning and swore an oath with one another; and Isaac sent them away, and they departed from him in peace. It came to pass the same day that Isaac's servants came and told him about the well which they had dug, and said to him, "We have found water." So he called it Shebah. Therefore the name of the city is Beersheba to this day" Genesis 26:26-33.

Abimelech the king of the Philistines had noticed that Isaac was flourishing in the land. Isaac had built a large enterprise with many employees and so he had become a force to be reckoned with. He came to Isaac to establish a covenant relationship. Covenant relationships establish the framework for peaceful coexistence. Instead of fiercely competing with one another, some enterprises choose to establish covenants with others. This is common in the airline industry where airlines have code-sharing agreements so that they do not necessarily have to compete on certain routes.

2

The Culture of Honesty

"You shall not bear false witness against your neighbor"
Exodus 20:16

America's struggle with sincerity, prejudice, unhinged rules and regulation dates to the foundations of the republic. The election of Abraham Lincoln, an anti-slavery republican in 1860, led to the seceding from the United States by some southern states to form the Confederate States of America. From April 1861 to May 1865, America fought a brutal civil war over the issue of slavery. The issue of slavery which led to the civil war was fundamental to the July fourth 1776 Declaration of Independence. One of the paragraphs of the United States Declaration of Independence states: "We hold these truths to be self-evident, that all men are created equal, that they are endowed by their Creator with certain unalienable Rights that among these are Life, Liberty and the Pursuit of Happiness." This same truth that all men are created equal is also enshrined in the Fourteenth Amendment which was adopted with the clause "no state shall… deny to any person within its jurisdiction the equal protection of the laws" into the Constitution in 1868.

The question is, why did America engage in a civil war over a fundamental truth such as the equality of humanity. Some have said that it was for political and economic reasons. It is important that we all come to terms with some basic truths from the scriptures about whom we are and why we are here as humans, to get to the root of systemic evils for which reasons we constantly perjure ourselves. On all the US dollar currency bills, it is boldly acknowledged that 'In God We Trust' and yet many of the laws and systems in the country are a departure from God's word.

Any government legislation, community rule, or corporate regulation that pivots away from the scriptures, sets up a framework for insecurity. Insecurity breeds perjury. People must have absolute confidence in the laws and systems by which the country and organizations are governed so they can become sincere. If the laws and systems of society are not hinged to the truth, people are only sincere when it is convenient. A sincere society is where there is faith in God, great confidence in human authorities as well as in ourselves. For many people who must endure the lingering backlash of systemic prejudice, altering information has become the way for sheer survival.

A typical instance is in the family where some parents who are accosted with unexpected questions from their children, tend to formulate answers which are often not accurate. Assuming these children discover that their parents lied to them, there is a breach of trust and worst of all a tampering with their fundamental value system. Being honest is the essence of the ninth commandment. Honesty means to be sincere, truthful, impartial and reasonable. A core truth about our existence is that the world was framed by God's word. The standard by which all truth anchors is the word of God. "Now faith is the substance of things hoped for, the evidence of things not seen. For by it the elders obtained a good testimony. By faith we understand that the worlds were framed by the word of God, so that the things which are seen were not made of things which are visible" Hebrews 11:1-3. Any information that is credible must provide full context, history, evidence and substance.

Context

American journalism formally began in 1690, when Benjamin Harris published the first edition of "Publick Occurrences, Both Foreign and Domestick" in Boston. Fueled by the campaign for independence, newspapers became popular in spreading information and press houses mushroomed after independence when the constitution guaranteed the freedom of press. With faster printing presses, telegraph, radio and television also came alongside. We are currently in the age of information where a lot is accomplished by leveraging digital technology. Several businesses are thriving today on the wings of ecommerce and we get most of the news today in real time via the internet. Today, it would be awkward for anyone not to own at least a cell phone. The New York Times, Wall Street Journal, CNN, CBS, ABC, NBC are prominent among several traditional news outlets. Alongside these traditional media houses is the advent of social media where anyone can post news for public consumption. Facebook, Twitter, Instagram and Linkedin are popular social media platforms. What was previously referred to as gossip and rumors are now known as 'Fake news' which is a term popularized by President Donald Trump.

In this information age, politics, business and communities thrive on the wings of good information. The news has been used as a tool for manipulating the outcome of elections. Social media has been used by political leaders to make significant announcements. Wall Street as well as other Stock Exchanges across the world hinge on real-time news. Social media marketing and ecommerce has emerged as a cornerstone for business success. The advertising revenues of Facebook for example, have catapulted the young company into a multi-billion-dollar enterprise. Effective mobilization for communal programs is done through the internet. Through the internet, millions of people are rallied for events such as solidarity marches, protests and counter protests.

While the information age has significantly accelerated development across all spectrums of life, there are also many challenges. Terrorism, cyber bullying, online pornography, misinformation are among several problems that have skyrocketed. The terrorist group ISIS for instance, was able to propagate its agenda and recruit people from across the globe through social media. Many young people have fallen victim to radicalization schemes through the internet. Unlike the traditional media which hinges on the standards of professional journalism, the strange attitude of most people is that once an information is posted on the internet it should be legitimate. 'Fake news' now passes for real news. Most often, illegitimate information comes in the form of sound bites. Though the posts of gossip or rumors are very short and lack depth, people are willing to make up the lacking pieces of the puzzle in their minds. Most people do not demand full context of a posted story before they start jumping to conclusions with 'like' comments. We have become a generation of 'itchy ears'. The Apostle James admonishes us, "So then, my beloved brethren, let every man be swift to hear, slow to speak, slow to wrath" James 1:19. It is important to receive information that is being communicated, but then we must not be hasty to react. We must seek the full context of a narrative as well as test the information before acting upon it.

At a point during the reign of King David, his son Absalom organized a revolt against him so King David went into exile away from Jerusalem. He deliberately stationed the priests Zadok and Abiathar in Jerusalem so they could relay any important information to him through their sons Jonathan and Ahimaaz. When Absaloms' counselor Ahithophel gave counsel for an ambushment against King David, Ahimaaz and Jonathan were the couriers who brought the information to David. At the end of the battle between the army of Absalom and the army of King David where Absalom was killed, Ahimaaz requested the permission to carry the news to King David. "Then Ahimaaz the son of Zadok said, "Let me run now and take the news to the king, how the Lord has avenged him of his enemies." And Joab said to him, "You shall not take the news this day, for you shall take the news another day. But today you shall take no news, because the king's son is dead." Then Joab said to the Cushite, "Go, tell the king what you have seen." So the Cushite bowed himself to Joab and ran. And Ahimaaz the son of Zadok said again to Joab, "But whatever happens, please let me also run after the Cushite." So Joab said, "Why will you run, my son, since you have no news ready?" "But whatever happens," he said, "let me run." So he said to him, "Run." Then Ahimaaz ran by way of the plain, and outran the Cushite. Now David was sitting between the two gates. And the watchman went up to the roof over the gate, to the wall, lifted his eyes and looked, and there was a man, running alone. Then the watchman cried out and told the king. And the king said, "If he is alone, there is news in his mouth." And he came rapidly and drew near. Then the watchman saw another man running, and the watchman called to the gatekeeper and said, "There is another man, running alone!" And the king said, "He also brings news." So the watchman said, "I think the running of the first is like the running of Ahimaaz the son of Zadok." And the king said, "He is a good man, and comes with good news." So Ahimaaz called out and said to the king, "All is well!" Then he bowed down with his face to the earth before the king, and said, "Blessed be the Lord your God, who has delivered up the men who raised their hand against my lord the king!" The king said, "Is the young man Absalom safe?" Ahimaaz answered, "When Joab sent the king's servant and me your servant, I saw a great tumult, but I did not know what it was about." And the king said, "Turn aside and stand here." So he turned aside and stood still. Just then the Cushite came, and the Cushite said, "There is good news, my lord the king! For the Lord has avenged you this day of all those who rose against you." And the king said to the Cushite, "Is the young man Absalom safe?" So the Cushite answered, "May the enemies of my lord the king, and all who rise against you to do harm, be like that young man!" Then the king was deeply moved, and went up to the chamber over the gate, and wept. And as he went, he said thus: "O my son Absalom—my son, my son Absalom—if only I had died in your place! O Absalom my son, my son!" 2 Samuel 18:19-33.

From the narrative, it is obvious that Ahimaaz did not witness the entire occasion of the death of Absalom. Joab the commander of the army initially denied Ahimaaz the permission to carry the news to the king. However Ahimaaz insists and outruns Cushite who had witnessed the entire occasion of the death of Absalom and was officially designated to convey the news to King David. When Ahimaaz arrived, the king quizzed him for specific details but Ahimaaz was unable to provide answers so the king told him "Turn aside and stand here." Ahimaaz was excused because he did not have the full context of the information he presented. Though Cushite came later, he was able to present the details required by the king. As human beings we are all designed to run with a message. Whatever we say or do at any point is a reflection of what information we are equipped with. It is our responsibility to get selective of the information that we accept as the basis for our running. In Isaiah 53:1, the scriptures say, "Who has believed our report? And to whom has the arm of the Lord been revealed?" The information upon which you run in life determines if God shows up to manifest his glory. Obviously if we run on falsehood, gossip and rumors, we become unhinged from the truth and do not expect God to be involved in our dealings.

History

One of the factors that make information legitimate is the background of a narrative. 'What is the story behind the story?' History is the bloodline of any information. It is important to investigate patterns and cycles that may have existed in the past with people, communities or occurrences.

"One generation passes away, and another generation comes; But the earth abides forever. The sun also rises, and the sun goes down, and hastens to the place where it arose. The wind goes toward the south, and turns around to the north; the wind whirls about continually, and comes again on its circuit. All the rivers run into the sea, yet the sea is not full; To the place from which the rivers come, There they return again. All things are full of labor; Man cannot express it. The eye is not satisfied with seeing, nor the ear filled with hearing. That which has been is what will be, that which is done is what will be done, And there is nothing new under the sun. Is there anything of which it may be said, "See, this is new"? It has already been in ancient times before us" Ecclesiastes 1:5-10.

While writing this book, NASA predicted an eclipse of the sun. "On Monday, August 21, 2017, all of North America will be treated to an eclipse of the sun. Anyone within the path of totality can see one of nature's most awe inspiring sights - a total solar eclipse. This path, where the moon will completely cover the sun and the sun's tenuous atmosphere - the corona - can be seen, will stretch from Salem, Oregon to Charleston, South Carolina. Observers outside this path will still see a partial solar eclipse where the moon covers part of the sun's disk."

I watched on television how the eclipse manifested through the exact path mapped out for its occurrence. The total eclipse occurred in Salem, Oregon and Charleston while those of us further away experienced a partial eclipse of some sort. Through historical patterns and cycles, Scientists were able to make an accurate determination of this occurrence. The timeline for the next occurrence is already published.

The sun in the sky above us, the winds, water bodies as well as how we act and react as humans are all an unending cycle. Good information is one that identifies with past trends. From the scriptures we learn the entire history of the earth from the creator. Holy men and Jewish scribes recorded events, God's role and perspectives by inspiration. The Jewish historian Josephus and Herodotus the Greek historian as well as many others provide us with information of occurrences in the past. Internet search engines like Google, Bing, Yahoo and Ask among others provide us with a great treasure of credible resources by which we can understand the backdrop of a narrative.

Many of the opportunities and privileges from the government or corporate world in America are made available by zip codes. Where you live may either qualify or disqualify you. Also when applying for most things from the government, corporations or institutions, we often have to fill in a questionnaire to provide our information. In several cases the information required are intrusive and used against applicants. In other words 'What you say, can be used against you'. People sometimes provide falsified information because they do not want to be denied the benefits they are seeking. The question here is, 'Is it possible to alter a pattern of behavior and can evil cycles be broken? Whenever there is repentance and transformation, patterns are altered and cycles are broken. While patterns are inherent behavior, cycles originate from external sources.

1. *Patterns* –

In the human context, this is a predictable manner of behavior. The dictionary defines it as a regular or repetitive form, order or arrangement. When we were unsaved, we lived according to the course of this world as children of disobedience. "And you He made alive, who were dead in trespasses and sins, in which you once walked according to the course of this world, according to the prince of the power of the air, the spirit who now works in the sons of disobedience, among whom also we all once conducted ourselves in the lusts of our flesh, fulfilling the desires of the flesh and of the mind, and were by nature children of wrath, just as the others. But God, who is rich in mercy, because of His great love with which He loved us, even when we were dead in trespasses, made us alive together with Christ (by grace you have been saved)" Ephesians 2:1-5. The devil cast a mold of disobedience, lust and wickedness for us when we were unbelievers. It is a mold that makes us patterned after self which is the hallmark of his existence. The core attribute of Satan is that of self-centeredness and self-will. Salvation through Jesus Christ ushers us into a new lifestyle of righteousness. We take up our cross and follow Jesus and exercise self-denial. The cross of Jesus Christ is the new mold by which our character ought to be patterned. "Therefore, from now on, we regard no one according to the flesh. Even though we have known Christ according to the flesh, yet now we know Him thus no longer. Therefore, if anyone is in Christ, he is a new creation; old things have passed away; behold, all things have become new" 2 Corinthians 5:16&17. The grace of our Lord Jesus Christ has been lavished upon us as believers and so we are empowered to demonstrate the righteousness of Christ in all areas of our lives. We cannot remain in molds that we have outgrown by reason of our salvation. The Apostle Paul admonished his protégé Timothy, "But avoid foolish and ignorant disputes, knowing that they generate strife. And a servant of the Lord must not quarrel but be gentle to all, able to teach, patient, in humility correcting those who are in opposition, if God perhaps will grant them repentance, so that they may know the truth, and that they may come to their senses and escape the snare of the devil, having been taken captive by him to do his will" 2 Timothy 2:23-26. We cannot argue for the sake of argument. We must not talk about everything that comes to our minds simply because we can talk. We cannot participate in every conversation for the sake of it. What we say and do crafts a narrative about us. Many of us do not realize that the storyline to our lives has a direct relationship with how people relate to us. Everyone who hears us or sees us, stores the narrative of our discourse in their minds and ultimately affects their 'running' concerning us. The cross of Jesus presents us with an opportunity to come out of molds that brand us after the image and likeness of the devil.

2. *Cycles* –

These are sequence of events that are repeated again and again. Through demonic covenants and curses, we may have inherited cycles of evil manifestations through the bloodline. A common instance is an infirmity that recurs in certain seasons to plague members of a family. Disobedience to God's word and lustfulness is the premise for demonic mandates. "Hear my voice, O God, in my prayer: preserve my life from fear of the enemy. Hide me from the secret counsel of the wicked; from the insurrection of the workers of iniquity: Who whet their tongue like a sword, and bend their bows to shoot their arrows, even bitter words: That they may shoot in secret at the perfect: suddenly do they shoot at him, and fear not. They encourage themselves in an evil matter: they commune of laying snares privily; they say, Who shall see them? They search out iniquities; they accomplish a diligent search: both the inward thought of every one of them, and the heart, is deep" Psalms 64:1-6. In this Psalm, King David is praying to God concerning the schemes of the enemy. Those in the occult conduct a search of which area of life we have violated God's word, so they can make that their mandate to perpetuate an evil cycle. If the devil can get us to fit into the mold of 'self' he leverages the elements to manifest cycles of evil against us. When the devil came against Job, the scripture says he used wicked people such as the Sabeans and Chaldeans, demons of sickness as well as the elements of fire, wind to attack Job's tranquility. It is only when we continue in the mold of 'self' that Satan had used to brand us in the past that we continue to experience demonic cycles.

"And you, being dead in your trespasses and the uncircumcision of your flesh, He has made alive together with Him, having forgiven you all trespasses, having wiped out the handwriting of requirements that was against us, which was contrary to us. And He has taken it out of the way, having nailed it to the cross. Having disarmed principalities and powers, He made a public spectacle of them, triumphing over them in it" Colossians 2:13-15. In Christ we have access to the New Covenant in the blood of Jesus. In any aspect of life where we notice cycles of demonic manifestations in our lives and family, we have the authority to break such cycles. The first step is to locate the redemptive scriptures in these areas of oppression. The second step is to seek to understand the pattern of life that gives demons the mandate to oppress us in that area of life. Third step is to come out of this mold and demonstrate the righteousness of God in Christ Jesus. Fourth step is daily confession of these redemptive scriptures in the name of Jesus. Finally, we exert our authority and bind the demons responsible in the name of Jesus. Summarily, a life style patterned after the cross, continual declaration of our redemptive covenant scriptures and binding devils in the name of Jesus breaks all cycles of demonic oppression.

In the same way we may have inherited evil patterns and cycles through the bloodline, we also inherit good virtues through the bloodline. The Apostle Paul writes in 2 Timothy 1:3-5, "I thank God, whom I serve with a pure conscience, as my forefathers did, as without ceasing I remember you in my prayers night and day, greatly desiring to see you, being mindful of your tears, that I may be filled with joy, when I call to remembrance the genuine faith that is in you, which dwelt first in your grandmother Lois and your mother Eunice, and I am persuaded is in you also." Notice that the Apostle Paul chronicles a unique virtue that Timothy inherited through the bloodline. His grandmother Lois demonstrated genuine faith which was also evident in his mother Eunice. When we faithfully carry our cross in Christ, the victory of the cross flows through our bloodline as an ancestral blessing to the next generation. The Apostle Paul admonished Timothy, "But you have carefully followed my doctrine, manner of life, purpose, faith, longsuffering, love, perseverance, persecutions, afflictions, which happened to me at Antioch, at Iconium, at Lystra—what persecutions I endured. And out of them all the Lord delivered me. Yes, and all who desire to live godly in Christ Jesus will suffer persecution. But evil men and impostors will grow worse and worse, deceiving and being deceived. But you must continue in the things which you have learned and been assured of, knowing from whom you have learned them, and that from childhood you have known the Holy Scriptures, which are able to make you wise for salvation through faith which is in Christ Jesus" 2 Timothy 3:10-15. Paul was deliberate about how he conducted himself in life. He demonstrated the cross of Christ in every way. His teachings, manner of life, purpose, faith, endurance of persecutions were all a reflection of the pattern of the cross of Jesus. Paul makes references to places like Antioch, Iconium and Lystra where he was persecuted for preaching the gospel and yet he did not give up on his mission.

- *Paul In Antioch* –

"On the next Sabbath almost the whole city came together to hear the word of God. But when the Jews saw the multitudes, they were filled with envy; and contradicting and blaspheming, they opposed the things spoken by Paul. Then Paul and Barnabas grew bold and said, "It was necessary that the word of God should be spoken to you first; but since you reject it, and judge yourselves unworthy of everlasting life, behold, we turn to the Gentiles. For so the Lord has commanded us: 'I have set you as a light to the Gentiles, That you should be for salvation to the ends of the earth.'" Now when the Gentiles heard this, they were glad and glorified the word of the Lord. And as many as had been appointed to eternal life believed. And the word of the Lord was being spread throughout all the region. But the Jews stirred up the devout and prominent women and the chief men of the city, raised up persecution against Paul and Barnabas, and expelled them from their region. But they shook off the dust from their feet against them, and came to Iconium. And the disciples were filled with joy and with the Holy Spirit" Acts 13:44-52.

- *Paul At Iconium* –

"Now it happened in Iconium that they went together to the synagogue of the Jews, and so spoke that a great multitude both of the Jews and of the Greeks believed. But the unbelieving Jews stirred up the

Gentiles and poisoned their minds against the brethren. Therefore they stayed there a long time, speaking boldly in the Lord, who was bearing witness to the word of His grace, granting signs and wonders to be done by their hands. But the multitude of the city was divided: part sided with the Jews, and part with the apostles. And when a violent attempt was made by both the Gentiles and Jews, with their rulers, to abuse and stone them, they became aware of it and fled to Lystra and Derbe, cities of Lycaonia, and to the surrounding region. And they were preaching the gospel there" Acts 14:1-7

- *Paul At Lystra* –

"And in Lystra a certain man without strength in his feet was sitting, a cripple from his mother's womb, who had never walked. This man heard Paul speaking. Paul, observing him intently and seeing that he had faith to be healed, said with a loud voice, "Stand up straight on your feet!" And he leaped and walked. Now when the people saw what Paul had done, they raised their voices, saying in the Lycaonian language, "The gods have come down to us in the likeness of men!" And Barnabas they called Zeus, and Paul, Hermes, because he was the chief speaker. Then the priest of Zeus, whose temple was in front of their city, brought oxen and garlands to the gates, intending to sacrifice with the multitudes. But when the apostles Barnabas and Paul heard this, they tore their clothes and ran in among the multitude, crying out and saying, "Men, why are you doing these things? We also are men with the same nature as you, and preach to you that you should turn from these useless things to the living God, who made the heaven, the earth, the sea, and all things that are in them, who in bygone generations allowed all nations to walk in their own ways. Nevertheless, He did not leave Himself without witness, in that He did good, gave us rain from heaven and fruitful seasons, filling our hearts with food and gladness." And with these sayings they could scarcely restrain the multitudes from sacrificing to them. Then Jews from Antioch and Iconium came there; and having persuaded the multitudes, they stoned Paul and dragged him out of the city, supposing him to be dead. However, when the disciples gathered around him, he rose up and went into the city. And the next day he departed with Barnabas to Derbe" Acts 14:8-20.

God's word remolds our lives to become patterned after the cross of Jesus and this is how we manifest the power of God. There would be a new storyline of victory and dominion in our lives if we start to fit in the pattern of the cross of Jesus.

Evidence

As a clear departure from the European style monarchies which functioned as dictatorships, America is a country that boasts of the 'rule of law'. Here, the word of the king alone does not make someone guilty of a crime, rather there must be acceptable evidence. Evidence means something that gives a sign or proof of the existence or truth of something, or that helps someone come to a particular conclusion. It is important that we pursue the 'burden of proof' before jumping to any conclusions with information. What are the various pieces that make up the core of a narrative? We have to take up each component and investigate them. Do they hold up to what they profess or represent? Are they facts that can be verified? Archaeologists have diligently researched and continue to excavate for most of the 'so called' controversial events recorded in the scriptures and ascertain their credibility. Amazingly, most of these controversies have been discounted by the discovery of hard evidence.

From the descendants of Noah with his three sons Shem, Ham and Japheth we learn of the table of nations which historians who have undertaken a study have affirmed as remarkably accurate. The table of nations is a record in scripture that tells of how the earth was populated after the flood that wiped out all humans with the exception of Noah's family. "Now this is the genealogy of the sons of Noah: Shem, Ham, and Japheth. And sons were born to them after the flood....... And children were born also to Shem, the father of all the children of Eber, the brother of Japheth the elder. The sons of Shem were Elam, Asshur, Arphaxad, Lud, and Aram. The sons of Aram were Uz, Hul, Gether, and Mash. Arphaxad begot Salah, and Salah begot Eber. To Eber were born two sons: the name of one was Peleg, for in his days the earth was divided; and his brother's name was Joktan" Genesis 10:1,21-25.

While the accuracy of this record amazes those who have undertaken to verify its authenticity, it underscores the fact that all humans originate from one family. Particularly interesting, is the record that one of the descendants of Shem was named Peleg – "for in his days the earth was divided." Prior to this, the entire land mass of the earth was one piece. The entire world map looks like a puzzle that is broken apart just like the scripture outlines.

Evidence is an important element of faith. Many miracles of Jesus were made possible because of the evidence of faith. "And again He entered Capernaum after some days, and it was heard that He was in the house. Immediately many gathered together, so that there was no longer room to receive them, not even near the door. And He preached the word to them. Then they came to Him, bringing a paralytic who was carried by four men. And when they could not come near Him because of the crowd, they uncovered the roof where He was. So when they had broken through, they let down the bed on which the paralytic was lying. When Jesus saw their faith, He said to the paralytic, "Son, your sins are forgiven you" Mark 2:1-5. Faith can be visible because it demonstrates works of trust. In this case Jesus saw the actions of these four men who uncovered the roof in order to lower their paralyzed friend into the presence of Jesus. They projected above the crowd blockage and removed the physical roofing barrier that impeded their access to healing. The effort of these four men was evidence of their faith in Jesus as the Son of God who could heal their friend.

The scriptures record another scenario in Mark 5:25-34, "Now a certain woman had a flow of blood for twelve years, and had suffered many things from many physicians. She had spent all that she had and was no better, but rather grew worse. When she heard about Jesus, she came behind Him in the crowd and touched His garment. For she said, "If only I may touch His clothes, I shall be made well." Immediately the fountain of her blood was dried up, and she felt in her body that she was healed of the affliction. And Jesus, immediately knowing in Himself that power had gone out of Him, turned around in the crowd and said, "Who touched My clothes?" But His disciples said to Him, "You see the multitude thronging You, and You say, 'Who touched Me?'" And He looked around to see her who had done this thing. But the woman, fearing and trembling, knowing what had happened to her, came and fell down before Him and told Him the whole truth. And He said to her, "Daughter, your faith has made you well. Go in peace, and be healed of your affliction." Notice that in this account also, the widow took steps that demonstrated her faith. She moved towards Jesus and defied the thick crowd. When she touched Jesus, there was an instant flow of power that healed her. Jesus attributed her healing to her tangible faith.

The Apostle James writes about the essence of evidence that substantiates faith. "What does it profit, my brethren, if someone says he has faith but does not have works? Can faith save him? If a brother or sister is naked and destitute of daily food, and one of you says to them, "Depart in peace, be warmed and filled," but you do not give them the things which are needed for the body, what does it profit? Thus also faith by itself, if it does not have works, is dead. But someone will say, "You have faith, and I have works." Show me your faith without your works, and I will show you my faith by my works" James 2:14-18. Our works of faith is a display of evidence. Evidence is the token of our faith which invokes the substance of manifestation.

Substance

Good information always tends to produce some benefit. Good information should educate, inspire, facilitate with opportunities and benefits we can all have access to. The purpose of good information is never to defame, deny or destroy but to facilitate goodness. "But without faith it is impossible to please Him, for he who comes to God must believe that He is, and that He is a rewarder of those who diligently seek Him. By faith Noah, being divinely warned of things not yet seen, moved with godly fear, prepared an ark for the saving of his household, by which he condemned the world and became heir of the righteousness which is according to faith. By faith Abraham obeyed when he was called to go out to the place which he would receive as an inheritance. And he went out, not knowing where he was going. By faith he dwelt in the land of promise as in a foreign country, dwelling in tents with Isaac and Jacob, the heirs with him of the same promise; for he waited for the city which has foundations, whose builder and maker is God" Hebrews 11:6-10. God rewards those who operate by faith. When we hinge ourselves to function in a framework of God's truths we demonstrate sincerity, fairness and justice with one another. The result would be a cordial atmosphere where everyone is properly rewarded for their honest efforts.

Based on divine revelation, Noah built an ark which preserved his family during the flood. Prior to this flood, there was no record of rainfall so the people of Noah's day probably ridiculed the idea that water will come down from heaven. The earth was one mass with all the continents fused together so there was really no need for a boat. Noah received divine specifications to build an ark which was also strange to his generation. However, truth is the basis of all substance, so when Noah built the ark as evidence of his faith, God substantiated this faith with the flood.

Abraham received a divine call to leave his country and family to go into the land of Canaan which God promised him for an inheritance. During his lifetime, Abraham was simply mandated to roam the Promised Land and envision it. Though he did not posses it in his lifetime, God entered a covenant with him and revealed some of the landmarks for the manifestation of the promise. A core landmark was that Abraham's descendants would be in Egypt for a period of four hundred years after which they would come out and possess the Promised Land. The scriptures tell us that out of hatred, Joseph a great grandson of Abraham was sold into slavery in Egypt by his brothers. Eventually seventy members of Abraham's family migrated into Egypt and lived there for four hundred and thirty years. In line with God's promise, Moses was empowered to lead the descendants of Abraham out Egypt with great signs, wonders and miracles. Ultimately through the leadership of Joshua, the descendants of Abraham inherited the Promised Land. Abraham's faith was substantiated. Any information that does not hinge upon truth, defames and destroys, while information that hinges on God's truth ultimately produces substance that brings us benefits.

10

The Culture of Desire

"You shall not covet your neighbor's house; you shall not covet your neighbor's wife, nor his male servant, nor his female servant, nor his ox, nor his donkey, nor anything that is your neighbor's"
Exodus 20:17

Trends in the media and entertainment industries often point to the direction of America's heart beat and desires. Fiction as well as nonfiction publications of crime sell off the shelves faster than progress reports. Youth and adults alike are obsessed with violent video games and extreme sports. With the advent of the internet, the appetite for pornography and online gambling has hit the roof!

I am an early bird kind of person, so I tend to travel in the mornings to attend to my work. It does not cease to amaze me when I stop at corner shops early in the morning for a cup of hot coffee and find people waiting in line to buy lottery tickets. Particularly interesting is the effervescence with which they dictate to the teller the tickets and numbers to be staked. What also surprises me is their ability to detect an abnormally in the tally with great precision. They are lottery mathematicians indeed! We cannot blame them, for that is their own way of getting a shot at the American dream, 'the pursuit of happiness'. In their minds assuming they win the lottery, they can finance all their desires and live like the stars!

Desire is the essence of the tenth commandment. It is our cravings, appetites, wishes and lusts. The dictionary defines it as a strong feeling of wanting something or longing for something to happen. Our desires are an open invitation to the spiritual realm and may either invoke God's presence or devils to fill up the atmosphere of the world around us. God sees and is responsive to our heart desires that lean towards Him. "Delight yourself also in the Lord, And He shall give you the desires of your heart" Psalm 37:4. In the same way, when the overall desires of people in a community tend toward self aggrandizement, devils are invoked into the atmosphere. For God to come through with revival, the atmospheric balance must tilt in favor of righteous desires. "Oh, that You would rend the heavens! That You would come down! That the mountains might shake at Your presence— As fire burns brushwood, As fire causes water to boil— To make Your name known to Your adversaries, That the nations may tremble at Your presence! When You did awesome things for which we did not look, You came down, The mountains shook at Your presence. For since the beginning of the world men have not heard nor perceived by the ear, nor has the eye seen any God besides You, Who acts for the one who waits for Him" Isaiah 64:1-4. In any community where the enemy has outrun with evil manifestations, things would only change if there is a desire for revival that outweighs covetousness.

Broken dreams and failed aspirations is the story for many people in America today. While there are approximately one-percent that are so rich and are currently engaged in a virtual race to 'trillionaire' status, the American dream has become an illusion to many. Habakkuk a prophet of Israel during the era of captivity in Babylon was experiencing the common hardship of the day but at the same time burdened with the level of covetousness and wickedness in society. Like most corporations today, those who were rich during the era of Habakkuk concocted all kinds of schemes by which they defrauded people to enlarge their enterprises. "Indeed, because he transgresses by wine, He is a proud man, and he does not stay at home. Because he enlarges his desire as hell and he is like death, and cannot be satisfied. He gathers to himself all nations and heaps up for himself all peoples. "Will not all these take up a proverb against him, and a taunting riddle against him, and say, 'Woe to him who increases what is not his—how long? And to him who loads himself with many pledges'? Will not your creditors rise up suddenly? Will they not awaken who oppress you? And you will become their booty. Because you have plundered many nations, all the remnant of the people shall plunder you, Because of men's blood and the violence of the land and the city, and of all who dwell in it. "Woe to him who covets evil gain for his house, that he may set his nest on high, that he may be delivered from the power of disaster! You give shameful counsel to your house, cutting off many peoples, and sin against your soul. For the stone will cry out from the wall, and the beam from the timbers will answer it. "Woe to him who builds a town with bloodshed, who establishes a city by iniquity! Behold, is it not of the Lord of hosts That the peoples labor to feed the fire, and nations weary themselves in vain?" Habakkuk 2:5-13.

Unhinged desires! For many of those who work on Wall Street and in the financial industry across America, life is all about maximizing opportunities to amass riches. Habakkuk tells of impending judgment for those who employ foul means to pile up riches. Such riches would not endure the test of time.

Habakkuk resolved to change his condition by the right approach. "I will stand my watch and set myself on the rampart, and watch to see what He will say to me, and what I will answer when I am corrected. Then the Lord answered me and said: "Write the vision and make it plain on tablets, that he may run who reads it. For the vision is yet for an appointed time; But at the end it will speak, and it will not lie. Though it tarries, wait for it; because it will surely come, It will not tarry" Habakkuk 2:1-3.

The first step of the prophet was to sort out himself. To have a genuine perspective of life, we first have to check our own alignment. He said "I will stand my watch and set myself on the rampart, and watch to see what He will say to me." In other words, he determined to incline himself to truth and then pray to know what God designed as his future. God answered him and told him, "Write the vision and make it plain on tablets, that he may run who reads it." The second step was to make a plan based upon the vision. Our aspirations must be hinged upon the wings of a divine vision. As Christians we must never lose sight of our ultimate destiny which is eternity. Like Christ, we are here on earth on a pilgrimage. In the same way that Christ came to fulfill God's plan, has ascended into heaven and sits at the right hand of God in eternity, so should we seek to know God's plan while on earth and desire the crowns of eternity.

Next, God told Habakkuk, "For the vision is yet for an appointed time; But at the end it will speak, and it will not lie. Though it tarries, wait for it; because it will surely come, it will not tarry." This third step is about fulfilling our goals within the framework of times and seasons. Prosperity is inevitable when we align our aspirations with a great attitude to execute God's eternal plan for our lives.

Aspiration

The dictionary defines aspiration as breath – drawing air into the lungs. It is also defined as directing one's hope towards an achievement. Consequently, we can describe aspiration as the oxygen we breathe in and carbon dioxide we breathe out. Aspiration is core to our existence. There was an interesting encounter between Jesus and someone who approached with a challenge. "Then one from the crowd said to Him, "Teacher, tell my brother to divide the inheritance with me." But He said to him, "Man, who made Me a judge or an arbitrator over you?" And He said to them, "Take heed and beware of covetousness, for one's life does not consist in the abundance of the things he possesses." Then He spoke a parable to them, saying: "The ground of a certain rich man yielded plentifully. And he thought within himself, saying, 'What shall I do, since I have no room to store my crops?' So he said, 'I will do this: I will pull down my barns and build greater, and there I will store all my crops and my goods. And I will say to my soul, "Soul, you have many goods laid up for many years; take your ease; eat, drink, and be merry."' But God said to him, 'Fool! This night your soul will be required of you; then whose will those things be which you have provided?' "So is he who lays up treasure for himself, and is not rich toward God" Luke 12:13-21. The prayer request of this man was that Jesus should touch the heart of his brother to give him a portion of their inheritance. It is not stated why his brother was denying him of a portion of the estate but then it could be that their father disinherited him or the brother was just being greedy. To the young man who requested that Jesus should intervene in the sharing of the family estate Jesus said: "Man, who made Me a judge or an arbitrator over you?" This underscores the fact that not all prayer requests are legitimate. Not every desire that is expressed through prayer may be answered by God. Furthermore Jesus said, "Take heed and beware of covetousness, for one's life does not consist in the abundance of the things he possesses." In other words some of our desires may demonstrate covetousness. Covetousness is the craving for illegitimate things. It is an unlimited and unrestrained appetite for worldly things. Jesus told the parable of the rich fool who decided to expand his storehouses to accommodate increase and spend the rest of his life in pleasure. God noticed his desires and passed a sentence, "Fool! This night your soul will be required of you; then whose will those things be which you have provided?" This rich man was self-centered and thought of gratifying himself only. There was no aspiration to help the poor with his riches and so God decided to take his soul so that others would have access to his piled up goods. Jesus places human aspiration in its proper context, "So is he who lays up treasure for himself, and is not rich toward God." Our aspirations must incline us towards God.

Attitude

In December 1903, the Wright Brother achieved the first powered, sustained and controlled airplane flight. Prior to that achievement, several inventors in the past like Leonardo da Vinci tried unsuccessfully to build an aircraft that flies like a bird over rivers, mountains and hills unhindered. It is recorded that Leonardo da Vinci spent a considerable time trying to understand the anatomy of the bird that could be adapted to make flight possible. Ultimately the design of the aircraft as we know today is based on the features of a flying bird.

Assuming there were no hindrances to aspiration, then everyone would be able to accomplish whatever they desire. All human aspirations are subject to the inhibition of natural limitations and barriers. While limitations are inherent, barriers are usually external to our existence.

Examples of limitation include infirmities, fear, lack of knowledge and skills. The Apostle Paul experienced such a limitation, "And lest I should be exalted above measure by the abundance of the revelations, a thorn in the flesh was given to me, a messenger of Satan to buffet me, lest I be exalted above measure. Concerning this thing, I pleaded with the Lord three times that it might depart from me. And He said to me, "My grace is sufficient for you, for My strength is made perfect in weakness." Therefore most gladly I will rather boast in my infirmities, that the power of Christ may rest upon me. Therefore I take pleasure in infirmities, in reproaches, in needs, in persecutions, in distresses, for Christ's sake. For when I am weak, then I am strong" 2 Corinthians 12:7-10. Limitations are not meant to prohibit our advances in life, rather they are a divine design to foster greater thrust to overcome external challenges.

Barriers are external challenges. Examples of barriers include wicked people who hinder us and deny us of our opportunities and benefits, extreme weather conditions as well as demonic activity. While in Egypt, the Pharaoh was the barrier to the freedom of the Israelites from bondage. When the Israelites were freed from slavery in Egypt the next barrier was the Red Sea. Lack of water, food and wars with opposing nations were subsequent barriers they had to overcome.

During the earthly ministry of Jesus, there was a scenario in the scriptures when Jesus was hungry and the fig tree in his path failed to produce fruit to meet His need. "Now the next day, when they had come out from Bethany, He was hungry. And seeing from afar a fig tree having leaves, He went to see if perhaps He would find something on it. When He came to it, He found nothing but leaves, for it was not the season for figs. In response Jesus said to it, "Let no one eat fruit from you ever again." And His disciples heard it... Now in the morning, as they passed by, they saw the fig tree dried up from the roots. And Peter, remembering, said to Him, "Rabbi, look! The fig tree which You cursed has withered away." So Jesus answered and said to them, "Have faith in God. For assuredly, I say to you, whoever says to this mountain, 'Be removed and be cast into the sea,' and does not doubt in his heart, but believes that those things he says will be done, he will have whatever he says. Therefore I say to you, whatever things you ask when you pray, believe that you receive them, and you will have them." Mark 11:12-14, 20-24. Jesus taught His disciples to leverage faith to remove mountainous barriers that stood as an obstruction in their way.

Animals are instinctive beings possessing attributes that define their character traits by which they overcome natural limitations and barriers to their existence. There are several scriptures that articulate such traits that also exemplify great human potentials.

"Behold, I send you out as sheep in the midst of wolves. Therefore be wise as serpents and harmless as doves" Matthew *10:16.* When Adam and Eve were expelled out of the Garden of Eden, it also marked the beginning of a new era where animals assumed either predator or prey status. We see these same attributes demonstrated in humans. Jesus told the disciples that he was sending them on a mission which positions them as sheep in the midst of wolves. Think of sheep heading towards a pond to drink water and then they spot a wolf lurking around the pond. The presence of this wolf becomes a barrier that prevents the sheep from accessing water from this pond. The mission of His disciples would be as though they were sheep in an environment of potential wolf predators. In any case, Jesus shows them how they would overcome such a predator, "Therefore be wise as serpents and harmless as doves." Though in the Garden of Eden

the devil uses the serpent on a perverse mission of deception, Jesus teaches that the true character attribute of a serpent is 'wisdom'. He admonishes the disciples that to overcome predator barriers they should operate in wisdom and yet employ the attributes of a dove which is peaceful in nature. I call this the principle of alternative attributes. Here, though you are inhibited by a particular attribute, you leverage another inherent potential to overcome a barrier.

"As the deer pants for the water brooks, so pants my soul for You, O God." Psalm 42:1. "The Lord God is my strength; He will make my feet like deer's feet, And He will make me walk on my high hills" Habakkuk 3:19. The Psalmist portrays the deer as an animal with an unusual thirst. It would travel great lengths to seek for a drink of water. Habakkuk the prophet describes the stamina of the deer by which they travel great lengths and climb to ascend great heights. When we combine both attributes of the deer, we discover the essence of persistent strength in seeking God at times when He seems so far away.

"Go to the ant, you sluggard! Consider her ways and be wise, Which, having no captain, Overseer or ruler, Provides her supplies in the summer, and gathers her food in the harvest" Proverbs 6:6-8. An ant is such a tiny and frail creature that is so unassuming. As a teenager my dad took us during holidays to his property which was an

undeveloped lot in the outskirts of the city. Common to the landscape were anthills some of which were gigantic structures considering the size of an ant. For ants, the feeling is probably like standing near a very tall story skyscraper. King Solomon counsels the lazy minded who complain of limitations to observe the leadership attributes of the ant. Ants leverage a team work spirit to harness seasonal opportunities for year round survival and general advancement.

"But those who wait on the Lord shall renew their strength; they shall mount up with wings like eagles, they shall run and not be weary, they shall walk and not faint." Isaiah 40:31. There is a uniqueness that distinguishes the eagle from other birds. While most birds fly with their wings to get to their destination, the eagle is known to soar. The eagle waits for a wind blowing towards its intended destination and yields its wings. Compared with other birds, the eagle achieves the greatest heights. The pursuit of purpose and destiny requires great strength. Inner tenacity is not enough. Like an aircraft built for a long haul, the design must incorporate aerodynamics as well as a strong engine. Aerodynamics means that the aircraft must make the best of the winds. In the face of good or bad weather, the aircraft must travel through and get to its destination. The engine of an aircraft provides the powerful thrust of movement. Turbulent clouds and weather storms can pose as external barriers to flight. Like the eagle, the aircraft has wings to navigate its

altitude. To avoid turbulent clouds, pilots would often manipulate the attitude of the wings of the aircraft to a clear altitude. From here we have the common saying that 'attitude determines altitude'. Regardless of our strength and determination to achieve divine destiny, we often become drained in strength if external forces of opposition constantly bombard us. This is why we are admonished to learn from the attributes of the eagle and seek God for divine strength in all our pursuits.

"The wicked flee when no one pursues, but the righteous are bold as a lion" Proverbs 28:1 – The lion is known to display majesty and strength. Its confidence is outstanding. The audacity to face the cross is what earned Jesus the attribute as the lion of the tribe of Judah. Similarly as believers we should not be intimidated by whatever the enemy confronts us with. We should employ the attribute of boldness because the Holy Spirit dwells within us to give us victory over all challenges.

Attitude is how we navigate ourselves to leverage inherent limitations and potentials to overcome external barriers in all realms of our existence. "And seeing the multitudes, He went up on a mountain, and when He was seated His disciples came to Him. Then He opened His mouth and taught them, saying: "Blessed are the poor in spirit, for theirs is the kingdom of heaven. Blessed are those who mourn, for they shall be comforted. Blessed are the meek, for they shall inherit the earth. Blessed are those who hunger and thirst for righteousness, for they shall be filled. Blessed are the merciful, for they shall obtain mercy. Blessed are the pure in heart, for they shall see God. Blessed are the peacemakers, for they shall be called sons of God. Blessed are those who are persecuted for righteousness' sake, for theirs is the kingdom of heaven. "Blessed are you when they revile and persecute you and say all kinds of evil against you falsely for My sake. Rejoice and be exceedingly glad, for great is your reward in heaven, for so they persecuted the prophets who were before you" Matthew 5:1-12. Jesus taught these nine beatitudes that potentially leashes our desires to God -

"Blessed are the poor in spirit, for theirs is the kingdom of heaven" – In the quest for supernatural power, some people turn towards the occult and become pompous in their ways. To be 'poor in spirit' is to desire the inspiration that only God provides.

"Blessed are those who mourn, for they shall be comforted" – There are many in society that are complacent with the spiritual decline and moral decadence. However, for those who are burdened, sense judgment and pray for divine intervention, Jesus says the Comforter will come through from above.

207

"Blessed are the meek, for they shall inherit the earth" – There are many who by their actions resist God and acquire their lustful desires by foul means. For those who submit themselves to God's dealings and do not resist His will, God will ultimately come through with the blessings of wealth and prosperity.

"Blessed are those who hunger and thirst for righteousness, for they shall be filled" – For many of the 'so called' enlightened in our society, their knowledge and experiences seem good enough to guide them through life. Jesus taught the need for the human heart to desire the righteousness of God in the same way the stomach craves for food. "But as it is written: "Eye has not seen, nor ear heard, nor have entered into the heart of man the things which God has prepared for those who love Him." But God has revealed them to us through His Spirit. For the Spirit searches all things, yes, the deep things of God" 1 Corinthians 2:9&10. The solutions to the deep socioeconomic and political challenges of the American society are neither in textbooks or annals of think tanks or institutions. The wisdom of God alone is the solution that comes as an in-filling of those who hunger and thirst for righteousness. On the Day of Pentecost, there was an outpouring of the Holy Ghost upon all those disciples of Jesus who waited in the Upper Room in Jerusalem. They were all filled with the Holy Ghost and were empowered to demonstrate awesome signs and wonders.

"Blessed are the merciful, for they shall obtain mercy" Self-centered people block the flow of riches and opportunities that should empower all in society. The merciful concern themselves with the mandate to change the condition of others and so God would consequently increase their capacity and bless their faithfulness.

"Blessed are the pure in heart, for they shall see God" — Living in the gall of bitterness and holding grudge against others, undermining and vilification are the hallmark of American politics, the corporate world and society at large. 'Washington is broken' is the term used to express the failures of the American government to work in a coherent way that fosters progress in society. The pure in heart are forgiving, kind, forbearing. Such virtues invoke the presence of God and allow His will to make an entrance into our hearts.

"Blessed are the peacemakers, for they shall be called sons of God" As I write this book, there is a deep controversy over clashes at protests with White Supremacist groups that recently took place at Charlottesville in Virginia. Conflicts and divisions would always arise in government, corporations and civil society at large. Firing people from their positions, dividing peaceful communities and families are never the best options. "Finally, all of you be of one mind, having compassion for one another; love as

209

brothers be tenderhearted be courteous not returning evil for evil or reviling for reviling, but on the contrary blessing, knowing that you were called to this, that you may inherit a blessing. For "He who would love life and see good days, Let him refrain his tongue from evil, and his lips from speaking deceit. Let him turn away from evil and do good; Let him seek peace and pursue it. For the eyes of the Lord are on the righteous, and His ears are open to their prayers; But the face of the Lord is against those who do evil" 1 Peter 3:8-12. Peacemakers are those who foster unity where there is division. In the face of crisis we must always work hard and seek to restore the tranquility.

"Blessed are those who are persecuted for righteousness' sake, for theirs is the kingdom of heaven" – Persecution of the righteous is the stock and trade of those who avail themselves to the devil. Though persecution is intended to discourage the righteous, those who endure it ultimately gain spiritual dominion.

"Blessed are you when they revile and persecute you, and say all kinds of evil against you falsely for My sake. Rejoice and be exceedingly glad, for great is your reward in heaven, for so they persecuted the prophets who were before you" – Throughout history we know that any new idea that challenges the status quo may come under intense attack by the established authorities. The Pharisees, Sadducees and Scribes in Jerusalem constantly challenged Jesus for his ministry and eventually got him crucified. Two

thousand years later, the verdict is clear, the gospel is still transforming lives and impacting generations of people.

You do not win a boxing contest with a defeatist attitude. There is a direct relationship that exists between the limitations within us and the barriers that accost us in life. Regardless of how huge and complex is the barrier that lies ahead, we have the potential to overcome. Assuming there is a barrier we have to overcome, the big question should be – What is the potential that lies within me by which I can overcome this? In the same way, the pilot of an aircraft would utilize the appropriate navigational system to manipulate the altitude of the aircraft to overcome a weather storm; if we can identify the limitation within us and leverage our divine potentials then we can readily leap over the related barrier. Attitude is how we navigate our limitations to overcome barriers.

Creativity

In the highly competitive environment of our corporate world, the quest for survival and expansion of market share pushes innovation to the edge. While some of the innovative ways are natural progressions for industries, others undermine the integrity of business. For the Christian believer, creativity and innovation is a legitimate blessing so long as one is functioning in the arena of their calling. The anointing furnishes us with the wisdom to remain on the cutting edge of creativity and innovation.

Beyond the instincts of animals, we as humans have the capacity for intellectual reasoning. Peter the apostle writes, "Grace and peace be multiplied to you in the knowledge of God and of Jesus our Lord, as His divine power has given to us all things that pertain to life and godliness, through the knowledge of Him who called us by glory and virtue, by which have been given to us exceedingly great and precious promises, that through these you may be partakers of the divine nature, having escaped the corruption that is in the world through lust" 2 Peter 1:2-4. Through the cross of Jesus, we have victory over the lusts that places limitations on us. We have been furnished with all that pertains to life and godliness. The power of God resides in us through grace so that we can operate as Christ did. We are endowed with the divine nature that enables us to pursue the promises of God for our lives. When Christ resurrected from death on the cross, God sent us the Holy Spirit on the Day of Pentecost. From then on, all believers have access to the Holy Spirit as an indwelling presence. Through the anointing we can walk with the Holy Spirit, ask questions which He answers so that we can make the best assessments and flourish in the pursuit of divine purpose.

To experience the fullness of the anointing, our thoughts must incline to truth. "Finally, brethren, whatever things are true, whatever things are noble, whatever things are just, whatever things are pure, whatever things are lovely, whatever things are of good report, if there is any virtue and if there is anything praiseworthy—meditate on these things" Philippians 4:8. Thoughts that are based on envy, jealousy and emulations are unwholesome and perverse. Such thoughts pervert our motives and block the conduits for the flow of the anointing.

Eternity

The ultimate design of our Christian faith is eternal life in Christ Jesus. "If then you were raised with Christ, seek those things which are above, where Christ is, sitting at the right hand of God. Set your mind on things above, not on things on the earth. For you died, and your life is hidden with

Christ in God. When Christ who is our life appears, then you also will appear with Him in glory" Colossians 3:1-4. We cannot afford to set our affection in a horizontal paradigm. Looking upward to heaven is the disposition to gain what comes from above. If we look horizontally we end up chasing what may gratify our fleshy desires but then with no eternal value. Jesus told his disciples, "Let not your heart be troubled; you believe in God, believe also in Me. In My Father's house are many mansions; if it were not so, I would have told you. I go to prepare a place for you. And if I go and prepare a place for you, I will come again and receive you to Myself; that where I am, there you may be also. And where I go you know, and the way you know." Thomas said to Him, "Lord, we do not know where You are going, and how can we know the way?" Jesus said to him, "I am the way, the truth, and the life. No one comes to the Father except through Me" John 14:1-6.

Our mission here on earth is a pilgrimage where we are tested through the austere conditions of this earth so that we can earn eternal rewards. Jesus told the disciples that his mission after the cross and ascent into heaven would be to prepare mansions for us. Everyone would receive a reward that reflects their diligence in walking by faith in Jesus. Whatever we achieve while here on earth by the grace of God would determine what we are blessed with to enjoy eternally. The next great awakening will come when our aspirations, beatitudes, creativity and the quest for eternity comes into divine alignment.

References

Worldly Principles, Lambert Dolphin,
Puritan Migrants, Great Awakening, Azusa Street
Revival - Online Encyclopedia, www.wikipedia.org
Federal Bureau of Investigations website, ucr.fbi.gov/
University of Michigan Law Department website,
www.law.umich.edu
Hebrew – Greek Key Word Study Bible by Spiros
Zhodiates
Wilmington's Guide To The Bible by Dr. H.L.
Wilmington
NASA - eclipse2017.nasa.gov/
Wright Brothers -
www.history.com/topics/inventions/wright-brothers

About the Book

The American society is a melting pot of almost all cultures and a microcosm of trends across the globe. Core to the founding of this nation are scriptural values that spurred the nation into world leadership both economically and politically. From Scholarly Theologians to Practicing Clergy, Christians and non-Christians alike, there are lingering questions about what should be upheld as relevant truth and what truths may have become obsolete with time. Are the Ten Commandments still relevant to our everyday lives?

In 'American Culture in Water, Blood, Oil and Bread', Ken unveils the spirit behind truths which may look punitive yet crucial to our well-being and prosperity as a society. The book teaches how the process of sanctification, consecration, and the anointing ultimately fosters manifestation of tangible blessings in our lives.

www.ingramcontent.com/pod-product-compliance
Lightning Source LLC
Chambersburg PA
CBHW060027100426
42740CB00010B/1629